The Change⁵

Insights into Self-Empowerment

Jim Britt ~ Jim Lutes

With

Co-authors

The Change[5]

Jim Britt ~ Jim Lutes

All Rights Reserved

Copyright 2015

The Change
10556 Combie Road, Suite 6205
Auburn, CA 95602

The use of any part of this publication, whether reproduced, stored in any retrieval system or transmitted in any forms or by any means, electronic or otherwise, without the prior written consent of the publisher, is an infringement of copyright law.

Jim Lutes ~ Jim Britt

The Change

ISBN   978-0-692-43158-0

Co-authors

Dr. Jin Kyu (Suh) Robertson

Leonie Newton

Rich Perry

Jennifer Ritchie Payette, MBA

Kay R. Sanders

DaKara Kies

Denise Needham

Dr. Carolyn L. Butler

Damiani Sekoulidis

Lauren Perotti

Deborah Crowe

Larunce Pipkin

Julie Anne Jones

Jeanie Cisco-Meth

Reginald F. Butler

Chris Marlow

Cheryl Ginnings

Jacqueline Haessly

Sandi Cohen P.S. & Ed Cohen RPh.

The Change is proud to support

Good Women International

Every 5 minutes, one American child (many as young as 10 years old) will be abducted and trafficked into the sex trade. 274 children a day. 100,000 each year. And that estimate could be low. The total current number of human trafficking victims in the US alone reaches into the hundreds of thousands and worldwide into the millions.

All profits from the sale of Amazon Kindle electronic books 1 through 4 are being donated to Good Women International, whose focus is on the prevention of sexual exploitation of young women and children. They support self-empowerment and educational programs worldwide designed to educate our youth to avoid becoming a victim. A recent successful project was an anti-trafficking curricula for our high schools which is now complete.

Enslavement is a reality. It is documented and it is real. The question is: What are we going to do about it?

To make a donation to Good Women International, a non-profit corporation, go to: www.SupportGoodWomen.com. All donations are tax deductible.

DEDICATION

This book is dedicated to all those seeking change

Foreword

Berny Dohrmann, Chairman of CEO Space International

To The Readers of *The Change* Series

Jim Britt has been a mentor to *Chicken Soup* authors, and to some of the foremost thought leaders on earth. Jim Britt's groundbreaking work in *Letting Go*, releasing past traumas and betrayals in life to return once again to forward-looking manifestation within your full powers, has been instructing at leading *Fortune* companies and to standing-room-only seminars all over the world. For three decades, Jim Britt has been the "trainer of the trainers," of which I am only one. Jim has been an instructor at CEO Space, the most prestigious, hard to get into faculty on the planet, where he developed millions of dollars of resources as he assisted others to develop tens of millions of dollars for their own dream making. Jim is the most "unchanged by success and wealth" man I have ever known. He is an unselfish archangel, like in his book *Rings of Truth*.

Today, Jim Britt and Jim Lutes, along with many inspiring co-authors from around the world, bring a pioneering work to the market to transform your own journey into master manifestation. Their principles are forged on coaching millions on every continent. As you read, you are exploring self-development as the world has yet to practice. In fact, Jim and Jim's publications lead to this one APEX MOMENT. Everything you have done to date in your own life, everyone you have met, every lesson you have learned, has led you to this one GREAT life opportunity... the moment of your own transformation into ever-rising full potentials.

As a five time best-selling author myself, as a filmmaker, and with CEO Space, you can imagine how fussy I am to write a forward to publications in the self-development space. CEO Space was just ranked by *Forbes Magazine* as the leading entrepreneur firm, which hosts five annual business growth conferences serving over 140 countries. It was also named by *Forbes* as THE MEETING in the world that YOU CANNOT AFFORD TO MISS. The world today demands more than a reputation defender to secure your forward brand; it requires that you take responsibility for your own brand and reputation in life. This book will inspire you to do just that.

CEO Space International has supported launches for many amazing works, including *Chicken Soup for the Soul; Men Are From Mars, Women Are From Venus; Rich Dad, Poor Dad; The Secret; No Matter What; Three Feet From Gold; Conversations With The King*; and now the movies *Growing Up Graceland* and *Wish Man* (for Make a Wish Foundation); *Outwitting the Devil* by Napoleon Hill and Sharon Lechter; Tony Robbins' great publications; of course Jim Britt's best-selling book *Rings of Truth;* and so many more. The totals have reached more than 2 billion eyeballs! You can't play around with that Mount Everest of credibility that I guard like a bank vault!

You can therefore appreciate why I encourage 100% of our followers of all the publications named to BUY JIM BRITT and JIM LUTES book series *The Change* as a customer recognition for your own ten-best close relationships or clients. But don't just buy this book, rather I endorse that you buy 10, and you giftwrap them to acknowledge your most important top ten relationships in life, or clients in business. By doing so, you will retain more clients and encourage repeat buying. You may also receive more referrals and strengthen each relationship. The laws of giving will come back to you 10 to 1. When you give freely, you will always receive a rain into your life just as you rain into the lives of those you treasure. Jim Britt, Jim Lutes, and the insightful and inspiring co-authors have given you in *The Change* series a great opportunity… more important than pouring ice water over someone's head on YouTube as a challenge for charity! The gift that keeps on giving begins when you step up and BUY 10, knowing you have been instrumental in inspiring 10 friends to live a better life. Together, we are going to reach 1 BILLION SOULS as we help Jim Britt, Jim Lutes, and their co-authors to achieve their goal to transform human consciousness in our lifetime. Like Zig Ziglar, Jim Rohn, the great Roger Anthony, and so many friends who have passed, my friend Jim Britt is now a historical event in every training, every publication, and every online work at CEO Space. If you ever have the opportunity, STOP YOUR LIFE and see JIM BRITT & JIM LUTES LIVE and you will thank me personally, I know.

Their work is powerful. You'll let go of the baggage you've been carrying around for years and learn to embrace everything that creates the future you want and deserve. As you close the pages of any of *The Change* books, you will say over and over again "THANK YOU Jim Britt and Jim Lutes for creating this work." You will gain a new life of super focus as never before and you will commence to master manifest in your own individual life as never before. *The Change* books provide tools to transform results for corporations, institutions, and individuals, and once applied it will be impossible to miss your future success in life.

In my opinion, there are only the following areas to embrace for each of us:

- Spiritual oneness and balance

- Recreational balance and nature

- Relationship where *Perfection Can Be Had!* (my book)

- Career attainment of goals that you, yourself reset along the way

- Parenting either directly or by embracing a child you adopt to mentor at any and every age in life

These perspectives come into alignment within a framework of Jim Britt and Jim Lutes' imagination, along with decades of human-potential work. My advice is this work is a "BUY 10 TO SHARE WITH FRIENDS" pledge. In fact, a billion readers is a global path that Jim Britt and Jim Lutes are going to achieve NEXT for the world common good.

Let's help in this quest, as both men unselfishly donate their only asset, their precious LIFE TIME, to elevate one life at a time to their full potential and greatness.

My final request to all those who are reading my forward is that you DO IT NOW. When you think of the good you will be doing, just ask yourself, "How long will I make them WAIT?"

I'm buying my 10 today!

Berny Dohrmann

Chairman, CEO Space International

P.S. I so approve this message for all my readers and followers worldwide. CEO Space has helped authors break the book of all records a half a dozen times, which means the only record to beat can be done with the publication you are buying 10 of now. Together we are going to set a global record with one publication. Make the PLEDGE and give the gift of personal development. DO IT TODAY!

Table of Contents

Foreword ix

Jim Britt : Unleashing Your Authentic Power 2

Jim Lutes: Adjusting the Mind... 12

Chris Marlow: Transformation through Niche Domination: A Proven Path to Success.. 22

Damiani Sekoulidis: An Open Letter to Western Women 36

Cheryl Ginnings: REPURPOSED, NOT reTIRED! 48

Deborah Crowe: Work–Life Balance Seen through the Eyes of a Renaissance Woman 61

Dr. Carolyn Butler: Breakdown to Breakthrough: Live Life Intentionally Courageous 75

Jeanie Cisco-Meth: Metamorphosis 86

Julie Anne Jones: Solving the Myth of "Overwhelm" Using The Triple D Approach 96

Rich Perry: Transform Pebbles into Mountains 106

Dr. Jin Kyu (Suh) Robertson: My Own Vision, My Own Dream 116

Leonie Newton: From Self-Loathing to Self-Loving................. 129

Kay R. Sanders: The Power of the Mind 141

Reginald F. Butler: Director's Cut: The Adaptive Mind-set 153

Larunce Pipkin: The Ghost in Your Machine 164

Lauren Perotti: Reach For the Light 174

Sandi Cohen, BS and Ed Cohen, RPh: Sliding Doors 187

Jacqueline Haessly: Transformation for a Culture of Peace 200

Denise Needham: Change with Purpose, Passion, and Power 212

DaKara Kies: How to BE Money 224

Jennifer Ritchie Payette, MBA: My Search for Authenticity 233

Afterword 245

Jim Britt

Jim Britt is an internationally recognized leader in the field of peak performance and personal empowerment training. He is author of 13 best-selling books, including *Cracking the Rich Code; Cracking the Life Code; Rings of Truth; The Power of Letting Go; Freedom; Unleashing Your Authentic Power; Do This. Get Rich-For Entrepreneurs; The Flaw in The Law of Attraction;* and *The Law of Realization,* to name a few.

Jim has presented seminars throughout the world sharing his success principles and life-enhancing realizations with thousands of audiences, totaling over 1,000,000 people from all walks of life.

Jim has served as a success counselor to over 300 corporations worldwide. He was recently named as one of the world's top 20 success coaches and presented with the best of the best award out of the top 100 contributors of all time to the direct selling industry. He also mentored/coached Anthony Robbins for his first five years in business.

Jim is more than aware of the challenges we all face in making adaptive changes for a sustainable future.

Unleashing Your Authentic Power

By Jim Britt

Do you remember a time in your life when you got what you wanted effortlessly? A day or an experience in which everything just flowed? You were in the right place at the right time with the right people, and everything just seemed to work out perfectly.

Would you like to discover how you can be in that flow more and more of the time? In other words, would you like to know how to shorten the time between the creation of your vision and the realization of that vision? If you knew that secret, wouldn't you then feel better about yourself and your life?

There are two primary things you'll need to achieve a more peaceful flowing life. They are "Attention" and "Intention." It is very rare that we give our *full* "attention" with *focused* "intention" to what we desire to accomplish.

Most of us instead spend at least a good part of our day going over internal dialogue. We relive past experiences, worry about the future, blame the outside world for our shortcomings, and criticize ourselves for not having all we want by this point in our lives. We do this both consciously and unconsciously. Even while we are listening to others, we aren't really fully present. Instead, we are rehearsing our answers, slipping back into yesterday, and worrying about tomorrow. Sound familiar?

When you live your life with *full* "attention" and *focused* "intention," you are operating within your authentic power. This is the state in which things happen with very little effort in a much shorter period of time. This is where you discover the answers to all of your questions and problems.

Think of a time when you were trying to remember someone's name, let's say in a movie you've seen. And as hard as you try, the name just doesn't come to you. You see their face, but no name. Then you finally say, "Oh well" and let it go. The next instant after letting go, the name comes to you. We've all had that experience.

Living in your "authentic power" means living fully and being totally present, and not trying so hard to force things into existence. Only when you are totally present can you open yourself up to the real power of your imagination and creation process. Create the vision, let go of the need to control the outcome, and when you do the answers will appear. Only when you are "in the moment" can you be open to receiving the opportunities and miracles that are all around you.

The reason the creating process take so long is because about 90% of our time is spent focused on problems, outside noise, and internal chatter rather than letting go of the need to control the outcome and allow the solution to appear. When you are focused on the problem, there is no capacity to receive a solution.

The reality is we are always using our imagination to create at every waking moment. Your daydreams, for example, are the use of your imagination. A daydream is the result of your imagination creating a vision of a real experience happening in the future… or reliving some past experience.

Mental visions are like languages. They are basically the patterns and structures that exemplify the thinking of the mind that produced them. Simply put: you can change the outer results of your life by changing your mental language paints, by seeing something in a new and different way. By changing your vision, and the way you think and express your thoughts, you can change your life's circumstances. This means that if you change a vision of the future, you also restructure the patterns in your life that are used to create it. In other words, by changing a certain vision, you also change all the connecting visions that kept your old beliefs alive. What I'm saying is that you can literally transform your outer world by rearranging your inner world.

You never stop creating. You are always and without question creating the realities of your visions. We all have visions of how we see ourselves in life. Your inner you, your beliefs, are always at work creating the outer you. Change the inner you and the outer you changes with it.

What about *your* visions; are they more about *what* you want and *why*, or more about what you *don't* want and *why* you don't want it? If you want to achieve something different in your life, you must take a look at what you are consciously creating and what belief you are holding inside that is creating it.

As you begin to become more "mindful" of your inner visions, your intention, and where you focus your attention, you will begin to strengthen and trust your own inner guidance. When you become more mindful, more self-observant of your inner visions, you start to see the truth behind your actions, and only then can you change the outer result. Seek to know yourself and you'll begin to discover ways of transforming outdated destructive beliefs into new productive visions supporting what's important in your life.

In my opinion, we try much too hard to accomplish what we want in life. We are taking life much too seriously and we're working much too hard at it. Life should be fun, don't you think? In my opinion, we all need to learn to lighten up a bit, be present with ourselves, and stop making everything such a complicated intellectual process.

Let your life flow and see what happens. Connecting with and utilizing your authentic power to create the life you want is a feeling process, not an intellectual process. When you begin to make the shift from intellectuality to feelings, a sense of ease and well-being will sweep over you in an instant.

We've all done enough "wanting" to last five lifetimes. We've tried enough intellectual techniques to improve our lives to last a lifetime. If all of that could have worked, it would have worked by now.

The fact is that someone somewhere along the way has convinced us that if something is going to be worthwhile, it's going to require a lot of hard work and you have to get serious about it. That type of outdated thinking is what stands in our way more than anything else. Knowing more and working harder to make life easier is not the answer. It's developing the understanding of how simple life can be and opening yourself up to the miracles in life, instead of trying to create your own miracles. You can't force anything into existence. You can't make a miracle happen. Create your vision, then let your imagination flow freely. When you do, answers will appear. That's the real miracle!

Look at the creation process this way; the whole universe is made up of energy waiting to be directed by you and me. It's energy that responds to your intentions. You are in partnership with that energy and can use it to create anything you want. All people are a part of this energy as well. This means that when you create a vision of something you want or you have a problem that needs solving, the right people will show up and circumstances will be influenced to bring forth solutions to accomplishing what you want. In fact, this process is at work in your life 100% of the time. Create struggle and focus on that and the answers will come to you to create more of the same. Remember, you are partnering with the energy to create anything you focus upon. What you hand out comes back.

In other words, the basic "stuff" of the universe at its very core is pure energy that is shaped by human imagination and intention. The question is what are you imagining and intending?

The intention we hold toward a given outcome causes our energy to be projected out into the world. This energy we project will attract other energy systems, who in turn offer us solutions to what it is we are projecting.

I'm not talking about the Law of Attraction. You don't attract things to you, but when you decide to have something in your life, your view of the world changes and the view the world has of you changes. In other words, your intention causes you to see things differently and those around you to see you differently. For example, if you decide to earn more money this year over last year, only then do you start looking for the opportunity to do so. When your view changed to earning more money, opportunities start to appear. You didn't "attract" those opportunities; you simply recognized them because of your vision and intention.

Have you ever had a vision of some course you wanted to take in your life and suddenly you met someone or saw something that led you directly to the opportunity you envisioned? It felt like destiny, didn't it? It felt as though you had been guided by some mystical power. This kind of experience gives you a feeling of excitement and mystery, and as a result you feel much more alive and productive. You have just connected with your authentic power, which only operates in the moment and to the degree of clarity of intention you hold toward your vision.

Challenge yourself to remain intentionally connected to your authentic power. Use your imagination. Create your intention. Let go of the need to control the outcome. Then let the day as it unfolds become your workshop. When others are uptight around you, learn to just relax into your own well-being and sense of confidence that everything is unfolding perfectly. Learn to simply step back and observe the dramas around you as they unfold and choose whether you want to be a part of them or not.

When a problem arises or you need a solution, simply stop for a moment before you proceed and ask yourself, "Is this action I'm taking moving me in the direction I want to go?" If not, just relax for a moment and be open for the right solution to flow to you and it will.

Getting into this flow is not an intellectual process, a moral concept, a technique, or anything else. It's an energy flow that travels so fast that it's everywhere at once. By staying reconnected to it, you can literally achieve immunity to what you *don't* want and harmony to what you *do* want in your life.

Many traditions, religions, and techniques express the idea that getting in touch with this sort of spirit aspect of ourselves is a long-term process involving great discipline and special techniques.

Discovering the spirit aspect of yourself is actually simple and easy. It has to be. Nothing is so intimately a part of you as your own spirit. It's who you are at the core and it is something that cannot be separated from you. It can't be lost, so you don't have to go somewhere to find it. It is the very essence of who you are. This part of you is where the creative process takes place.

We seek joy and happiness in our lives because joy and happiness are our true nature; otherwise, why would we strive so hard to find it? Being able to live and operate from this level will bring you complete fulfillment in every way. However, this can only happen when you let go of the need to control outcomes and resolve the layers of conflict within. When we resist the flow of life by hanging onto our old perceptions, what we are actually resisting is having joy and happiness in our lives and struggling for what we want. We are resisting life as it should be. This isn't mystical at all. It's actually pretty simple when you think about it.

Attempting to earn happiness through behavior or material things will always end in failure, because as soon as you stop the behavior or get the material thing, you are right back where you began.

Experiencing happiness is beyond behavior. Search inside. Peel back all the layers of anxiety, doubt, fear, and anger and you'll discover the most basic truth of all—happiness comes from you, not at you.

The people of the world have created many false beliefs. Some say, "My way is better than your way." "Your savior is not *my* savior." "My heaven is different from yours." "My religious beliefs are right, therefore yours must be wrong."

Here's the simple truth as I see it. All life is one life. There is only one game in progress here on planet Earth and we're all playing the same game. We've just created different rules to play by. And all the games can work together if we don't judge the other's rules.

There are no races or differences in people, only different shades of skin. We fight wars in the name of God and religion. We even disagree on what day, what ritual, and even what building.

Truth is truth. If you help someone, you help yourself in return. If you hurt someone, you hurt yourself in return. It's that simple. If you share love and happiness with another human being, you increase the love and happiness energy within yourself. You don't have to believe me, just try it and see how it makes you feel. Everyone is made of the same material… energy. It's only the love in our heart and our intention that makes us different.

If you continue to view your life as if it were a problem, or if you continue trying to escape your imaginary problems or to blame others for your problems, your true nature will always remain hidden. However, even though it is hidden, you can rest assured it is always with you. Waking up to who you are requires letting go of that which you imagine yourself to be.

So, how can we shorten the time from "vision" to the manifestation of that vision? Just remember to stop as often as necessary to reconnect…to re-fill. Keep yourself in your authentic power by letting go of what disempowers you. This is where the action is. This is where your power to create exists. No one or nothing can take your power from you. Only you can choose to keep it hidden.

---

www.JimBritt.com

http://PowerOfLettingGo.com

http://CrackingTheRichCode.com

http://FaceBook.com/JimBrittOnline

http://JourneyBeginsNow.com

Jim Lutes

Having taught his branded form of human performance since the early 1990s, Mr. Lutes has accelerated top level entrepreneurs throughout his career by conducting trainings on personal growth and subconscious programming into worldwide markets.

During this time, Jim took his skills regarding the human mind, and combining it with trainings on influence, persuasion, and communication strategies, he launched Lutes International in the early 1990s. Based in San Diego, California, Jim has taught seminars for corporations, sales forces, individuals, and athletes. Having appeared on television, radio, and worldwide stages, Jim's style, knowledge, and effectiveness provide profound results.

"Jim Lutes possesses a unique ability to create performance change in an individual in a fraction of the time it takes his competitors." The core of humans decisions are based on the programs we acquire, reinforce, and grow. Combining Jim's various trainings, individuals can reach new levels of achievement and fulfillment in all areas of life. The results are at times nothing short of astonishing.

"My goal is to take that embryonic greatness that exists inside every person in America, foster it, empower it, and then hand them personal strategies based on solid principles that allow them to take that new attitude and apply it to creating a life by design."

Adjusting the Mind

By Jim Lutes

You are the one you are with, 24/7, 365. Your internal influence is so fundamental to how you operate in each moment. The question now becomes, how do you actually adjust your mind so that you can achieve optimum functioning on a daily basis? In fact, not just optimum functioning—all-out full-on vitality and achievement, daily, across all facets of your life! For this we have to turn to subconscious mind programming techniques. It is in adjusting the mind that you will truly be able to adjust your world. The more effort you begin to spend on using the techniques I am about to share with you, the more you will see results. You will see your life change in amazing and unthinkable ways, and much more swiftly than through using any other personal development techniques. You will see your life change on an entirely new level, and not only will you be creating change, but you will be creating sustainable change for your life. Who doesn't want that? What I am offering is not a quick fix, but it is a long-term and highly effective fix. Go for the long game—it always pays off.

By now, you get that your mind has two major players: the conscious mind and the subconscious mind. Your subconscious mind is like your GPS system, constantly running in the background. You conscious mind is like the steering wheel in the car. For many of us, we think we can take our hands off the steering wheel and let the car drive. What happens when we do this? Our GPS takes over and all of a sudden, all of those old limiting patterns, beliefs, and emotions take control. You may be driving along in life, feeling okay, when something happens, you take your hands off the wheel, your subconscious is triggered, and you are terrified or anxious without any understanding as to why. This is what happens when you are not in control of your conscious mind, the steering wheel of your life.

It is to live your life with awareness, and this applies even more so when you want to start adjusting your mind. You must be aware. We do so many things in a day—brush our teeth, clean our bodies, prepare nourishing meals, you name it—to keep ourselves presentable and healthy. There are all kinds of little things we do daily in the name of hygiene or keeping ourselves in good shape. Yet I have seen so many people—too many, in my opinion—who completely neglect their mental and emotional health! We take such good care to look good and feel good physically, but spend no time cultivating sound mental and emotional health. So you have to be aware of your thoughts and how you think, and integrate some techniques into your life daily if you want to truly make some changes.

Living life unconsciously, that is, letting your subconscious run along as it will, operating 24/7, and using your conscious mind to survive, will only lead to a life unfulfilled. This is a life that is mapped by continually looping and tripping on old habits and patterns. If you truly understand that within you is the power to do whatever you want in your life, then you will start to make it a priority to work on reprogramming your subconscious mind so that you can, in effect, get out of your own way.

Through these world-class subconscious reprogramming techniques, I will help you to get your subconscious functioning like a GPS that is your best buddy—your most potent ally! With some adjustments and fine-tuning, you can be rid of all the limiting stuff and position yourself to get on with it—creating your life as you really wish it to be. Just like eating the right things will contribute to good health on the physical level, so does thinking the right things contribute to good health on the mental and emotional levels. Being aligned in all areas of your life allows you to thrive completely. You can launch yourself out of survival mode and into thriving when you adjust your subconscious mind.

I want to share two simple techniques with you for adjusting the mind, but before I do, I want to impress upon you the importance of controlling the environment around you. It is not only your internal environment that is influencing you in each moment; indeed, the external environment is highly influential as well.

There are three ways the mind has been programmed. There is programming by authority, by traumatic incident, and by repetition. Inherent in each of these is the importance of environment. If you really want to expedite reprogramming your subconscious mind, it is imperative that you pay attention to the environment around you.

For instance, say you really want to get in shape. You work pretty hard at it, going to the gym an hour a day. Chances are you will be more motivated to stay disciplined and work hard at it if you are surrounded by people who are in good shape and stay active. If you find that your friend group is mostly made up of people who are overweight and choose sedentary activities over being active, you might find it more difficult to get into shape. That environment is not conducive to you being in great shape and is counterproductive in moving you towards your goal of being in great shape.

If you are driving a car down a road and the road is doing nothing but kicking up dirt and sand on the windshield, you might consider driving down a different road. It is as simple as that. Anything in your external environment that is not contributing to the desired end-result, anything that is not in alignment with your goals, must be changed.

This becomes a challenge when we look at the people in our lives. The people in our lives make up our interactive environment. You can and must control your interactive environment. It is imperative that you be selective and discerning about the people that you spend time with. Consider the role of the bouncer. Other people have a huge influence on us, and how we think about ourselves. You may have friends and family that are loving and supportive. These people emotionalize the feelings of love and encouragement in you. Look at whom you spend time with on a regular basis. Are these people positive or are they critical? You may have friends or family that try to hold you back, that are negative or criticize you constantly. These people are detracting from your environment and impacting your ability to get what you want. This is when the tough decisions have to come in—one of which might mean moving away from these people, or decreasing the amount of time you spend with them. If you cannot physically get space from toxic people, you can just tune them out. Turn the volume down in your mind's ear so that you no longer hear the negative comments. Turn the volume up once something positive to your ears appears. Keep in mind that like attracts like and try as much as you can to control what you take in at the auditory and visual levels. Work with the idea of feeding and nourishing your goals and dreams by choosing and creating an environment that supports them. You want to build an external map that helps cue you and reminds you of what your desired results are as you are building the internal map that will attract more things to support that which you want to manifest.

Another part of the environment around you is the spatial environment. You can control the space you are in to some degree, although not completely. However, controlling your spatial environment to be conducive to reprogramming your mind might look as simple as keeping an inspiring talk on your phone to listen to every time you get in the car. Turn your car into a rolling university—especially if you commute and spend anywhere from one to four hours in the car daily. Think about all the people who attend night school in the evening for two hours each week. If you drive two hours daily, you can educate yourself in that time by listening to personal development talks, audio books, inspirational audio, or why not learn a new language? This is one way to control and influence your spatial environment. Listening to soothing and peaceful music can also support a sense of relaxation and peace. It can directly affect your sense of place in your environment.

What if you are at home? What can you control in the spatial environment there? You can control what you watch on television, for example. Do you want the last images you see before bed to be violent or negative? (And this is especially important, because in a few paragraphs I'll introduce a technique you can use at bedtime.) Discipline is essential when controlling the spatial environment. How fast do you want to get into your life masterpiece? If you choose to watch television, choose to watch things that serve your highest interests. When you make choices throughout the day, keep the question "Is this moving me toward my life masterpiece?" in mind and let it help you make good choices. Then look around at all the things you can do to create a spatial environment that is conducive to moving you forward and reprogramming your subconscious mind.

Don't forget to control the internal environment by watching what you think and say to yourself. Watch your self-talk and replace negative thoughts in the moment. For example, if you find yourself thinking, "I am broke," replace the thought immediately with a positive one, such as "I am wealthy." Think about all of the ways and areas in your life in which you feel wealthy. For example, you may have excellent health, you may have a group of excellent and supportive friends, or you may have a wealth of ideas and inspirations. There are many different expressions of wealth and abundance! If you are using coupons to pay for things, make sure you are using them in the spirit of gratitude and abundance. Don't sit there cutting coupons and repeating to yourself, "I'm so broke, I have no money." Rather, use the coupon and say "Thank you" when you do. Turn saving money into a gratitude practice. When I get a bill for the phone, I say "Thank you!" every time. I thank the company for trusting me enough to provide me the service before I pay the bill. This kind of thankfulness keeps me focused on abundance and gratitude, whereas a response like "Ouch! This bill is high!" only keeps us in negative emotion—predominantly that emotional heavy-hitter, fear.

Another aspect of environment that you can control is what I call the 'incremental environment.' Have you ever been waiting for someone who was running late, and thereby found yourself with an extra fifteen minutes free? What did you do in that time? Instead of being cranky that your friend was late, I suggest you use that time in a productive way. Just like in your car, keep interesting and inspiring audio on your phone perhaps, or a book or a notebook handy. Use the fifteen minutes to develop yourself and continue this work. Don't think that fifteen minutes is not enough time to do anything! Whenever I have to pick someone up from the airport and they are late, I get excited. I get excited because I know that, in those moments while I am waiting, I can listen to or read something that progresses me further along in my personal development. I can continue growing while I'm waiting. You can become your own best project as you take these moments and utilize them with incremental space programming. Every incremental space, every unexpected 'extra' amount of time can be transformed into a learning opportunity, into a chance to revisit and re-connect with your dreams, goals, and desires.

Now, keeping in mind this aspect of controlling your external environment, let me introduce you to one basic technique for reprogramming the mind. I want to emphasize basic here: Imagine that reprogramming the mind is like karate. When you learn karate, you learn the basics first, like kata. You don't go straight into breaking boards. So it is with reprogramming the mind. Think of this technique like a basic building block of reprogramming the subconscious. As you begin to use such techniques with regularity, you will start to develop a conditioned response. In essence, we are trying to stretch the muscles of our mind, and do this repeatedly so they take new shape and don't contract back to where they once were. Look at a good guitar player—they can still play the guitar while singing, or talking, or smoking. They are not looking at their fingers; their fingers know where to go. Because they have practiced and practiced, they don't necessarily have to think about where to place their fingers for songs they have played forever. This is where we want to get your mind to: A place where your mind is newly conditioned and reprogrammed for positivity, success, or whatever it is you are moving towards.

So what are we waiting for? Let's get into the technique!

Our brains go through different states throughout the day; generally alpha upon waking up, beta throughout the day, theta when relaxed and heading to sleep, and delta when we are in deep sleep. The technique I will share with you is to be done while in the alpha state. How can you access the alpha state? This is the state you are in when you first wake up. Try this tomorrow morning—just wake up and be aware of those first moments of awakening. You might notice you hear the birds outside, or perhaps the sound of their chirping infiltrated the end of your dreams. Before you get up and get out of bed, take a moment in this state and just prop yourself up in your bed. Pick one subject and picture exactly how you want your life to look if that subject—money, a person, amazing health—were in your life. Now, remember that the subconscious cannot differentiate between reality and fantasy, and particularly so while you are in the alpha state. To sequence and secure the desired outcome, picture it while you are in this state. For example, say you want a black Mercedes-Benz. In the morning, just as you are waking up and still in the alpha state, picture this Mercedes-Benz exactly as you want it.

A quick explanation before we go on. When we are talking about reprogramming the subconscious mind, you may read or hear the terms 'associated' and 'disassociated' state. A simple way to distinguish between the two is through the following example. Imagine yourself on a rollercoaster and really picture yourself on that rollercoaster and seeing it through your eyes. This means you might see the bar, the seat, the view, and your legs and hands. This is an associated state. Now, imagine you are on the rollercoaster, but you are watching yourself on the roller-coaster as if you were in a movie. This is being in a disassociated state.

To really be effective in manifesting your desires in the alpha state, you have to picture what you want from the associated perspective. So, back to the Mercedes. Picture the Mercedes exactly as you want it—and include yourself in it. By using this technique in an associated state, we are emotionalizing the experience. Adding the emotion to the experience is like pouring gas on the fire, and it will instantly accelerate change in the subconscious mind. Remember that the subconscious does not differentiate from fantasy and reality, and seeks to provide that which you call to mind. The subconscious mind is like the seat of our golden ability to attract all of the things we want. To effectively print this car onto your subconscious mind, you need to process the idea through each of your senses. Remember, the subconscious mind understands everything through sight, sound, smell, touch, and taste. Picture the Mercedes and then build on this visual by seeing the car through your own eyes as you walk around it. Then reach out and touch the car as if you are actually there. This generates a tactile response in the alpha state. Picture yourself reaching for the door handle and opening the door of the Mercedes. Sit in the seat and feel the leather. Relax in the seat and call to mind the smell of the leather—this will add an olfactory (smell) response to the visual. Then, imagine you are turning on the music and hearing your favorite song—now we have an audio response to add to the olfactory and visual programming around the Mercedes. While you are relaxing in your bed, picturing all of this, visualize yourself relaxing in the car with the seat reclined. Imagine now that you are starting the car, and feel the anticipation and excitement. Remember—what is expected tends to be realized. Keep going with this visualization as you start the car—the car is fast and exhilarating. Point the car somewhere safe, push the accelerator down, and experience the car fully and completely!

What is happening in an exercise like this—whether you are thinking about a Mercedes, or the love of your life, or a fantastic body—is that these experiences in your mind are creating neural pathways in your subconscious mind, and your subconscious mind cannot differentiate between what is imagined and what is real. Your imagination is the co-pilot to engineering each of the things you wish and dream for.

Try doing this every morning for a minimum of twenty-one days without judgment or analysis. Just do it and hold it loosely, allowing it to happen as it will. Repeating this exercise for twenty-one days will create a new response in your neural pathways. This will in turn initiate an exchange that will create situations and interactions that will eventually bring the Mercedes to you. Everything manifests in circumstances and coincidences—it is always a series of events that brings these things to you. As you become in tune with yourself, all will change and your life by design becomes your reality.

To contact Jim:

Email: info@lutesinternational.com

Websites: www.lutesinternational.com and www.jimluteslive.com

Chris Marlow

Chris Marlow spent the first two decades of her career writing copy and making millions for big brands like Toyota, Nike, Disney, and Dell Computer.

Now Chris helps individuals discover that place in the business world where they're a perfect fit, and then shows them how to use powerful marketing tactics to reach their goals of client acquisition, passive income, and business building. Chris shows copywriters, coaches, info-marketers, and other service providers how to become a dominant force in their niche.

In 2010, Chris was diagnosed with invasive Triple-Negative breast cancer. The prognosis didn't look good.

A former coaching student introduced Chris to hypnotherapy and guided imagery. After some very strong work in this area, Chris opted for a double mastectomy. Three days later, Chris' doctor said, "We sliced and diced and could not find *any* trace of the cancer."

Today Chris offers a complete System for Success that includes resources for niching, copywriting, marketing, strategy, productivity, coaching, and hypnotherapy for removing blocks and setting intentions.

Chris' gift is being able to see *your* gifts and match them perfectly to an awaiting universe. Her focus on Niche Domination takes you to your highest potential in both earnings and career satisfaction.

Transformation through Niche Domination: A Proven Path to Success

By Chris Marlow

It's haunted me for years…

…a short story I was assigned to read in my literature class some 30+ years ago. I can't remember the author or the title, but I remember what happened.

It's nineteenth-century Europe. A peasant couple is working the coalmines. Oversight by management is brutal…almost like being in a Nazi concentration camp. Yet on their brief breaks, this couple fashions a magnificent statue out of mud.

A conversation between two managers ensues. One remarks on the exquisite beauty of the piece and suggests this couple should have a higher calling. The other agrees to their merit, but disagrees to elevating their status.

The profound sadness of this story (for me) comes from the squelching of human potential…not only for the two unfortunate peasants, but also for what was stolen from the world.

Our Gifts Should Not Be Squandered

In today's more enlightened environment, there is greater opportunity to share our gifts. Yet many fail to do so. Of those who do, most of them share their talents, wisdom, and creativity on a small scale.

The talented musician tutors one-by-one. The Internet marketer nurtures a tiny list. The writing coach helps 48 people per year, year in and year out, and never more.

Yet if you would talk with individuals who service others, most would say that they dream of bigger goals. The tutor would like a full classroom, the marketer would like a bigger list, and the coach would be thrilled to step up to group coaching and live events.

But what's holding them back? Very often, it's simply a lack of marketing knowledge, which breeds insecurity. The consequences echo the fate of our peasant sculptors. If you're not able to share your gifts abundantly, then abundance can't find its way back to you.

It's a well-known fact that "the more you give, the more you get." And that "what goes around, comes around." People like Tony Robbins, Jack Canfield, and Deepak Chopra prove that the more people you're able to help, the more the universe rewards you. And who wouldn't want more blessings, more love, and a richer harvest?

What follows are some observations from my 30+ years as a direct response copywriter and 13 years as a marketing coach and mentor. If you're a heart-centered solopreneur who is ready to help more people by expanding your imprint on the world, it is my goal to share some (perhaps surprising) wisdom that will motivate you toward your next steps.

The Truth About Competition

Some years ago, I read Timothy Ferriss' *The 4-Hour Workweek*. In it, he made a statement that stuck with me.

He said, "The fishing is best where the fewest go, and the collective insecurity of the world makes it easy for people to hit home runs while everyone else is aiming for base hits. There is just less competition for bigger goals."

The Change[5]

This statement struck me because it's true, and not only is it true, but anyone can hear the truth of it with their own ears.

According to experts, the average toddler hears the word "no" 400 times each day. For most people growing up, the phrase "you can't" is far more prevalent than the phrase "you can." Shad Helmstetter, author of *What to Say When You Talk to Yourself*, says that by the time we're 18 years old, we've heard the word "no" or the phrase "you can't" 148,000 times.

Negative input and limited thinking begets negative input and limited thinking and because of this, many begin their careers with lowered expectations, without even realizing it. Thus success on a big scale is for "others."

Those who find their way into the world of self-improvement are quickly taught by books and mentors that the first step to success is undoing the damage that's been done. This requires a repetitive "retraining" of the subconscious mind to replace the negative beliefs that hold you back with positive beliefs (and feelings) that let you manifest your desires.

Self-improvement icon Zig Ziglar tells an entertaining story that illustrates the power of repetitive reinforcement…

Two elephants were chained to keep them in place. The adult elephant had a very weak, small chain, but the baby elephant had a very large chain.

A puzzled onlooker asked the handler, "Why would you have a large chain on the baby but a tiny chain on the mother, who could easily break free?" The handler replied that the baby will fight the chain until he realizes that it is futile. The mother has already learned this.

The point of this section of the chapter is to illustrate that because so many people are programmed to underperform, excelling in your marketplace does *not* take a "quantum leap" on your part.

When you know the truth about competition, it makes it easier to believe you can accomplish very large goals—and *belief* is what makes it happen.

True Empathy: The Real Attractor Factor

To experience a substantial positive transformation in your business, you must ask yourself one question: "How well do I identify with my target audience?"

Because the degree to which you "connect" with your audience is the degree to which you will succeed in your business.

People buy from people they know, like, and trust. In *Influence: The Psychology of Persuasion*, Robert Cialdini makes the point that *liking* is one of the most powerful marketing tactics of all.

So if people *like* people who are "like" them, then one of the most effective things you can do is target (or create) a niche where your prospects are the mirror image of you. For instance, I am a marketing coach. Therefore, entrepreneurs naturally gravitate to my coaching program. I do not have to "sell" very hard and my mailing list grows naturally.

Now on the other hand, because I'm also a direct response copywriter, I can teach dentists how to get clients. In fact, I've written lots of copy for dentists over the course of my career. But should I become a teacher of dentists?

It's not advisable...because I've never *been* a dentist. I don't share his reality...I can't connect with him on a deeper level...we are not professional "siblings."

When copywriters write copy for their clients, they are required to have "empathy" for the client's target market. The degree of empathy that the copywriter is able to develop for the people in a target market will, in large part, determine how well the campaign will do.

The best copywriters *come from* the market they're targeting...they're software buyers turned software copywriters; they're stock and bond traders turned financial copywriters; they're alternative health fanatics turned health copywriters...they're entrepreneurs writing for entrepreneurs, and so on.

When you've walked a mile in someone else's shoes, you gain True Empathy. Possessing True Empathy for a *like* target market is the REAL Attractor Factor.

The Secret Sauce of Superstars

Stop for a moment and think of the superstars in the niches you follow. What do they all have in common?

Without a doubt, they all have great copywriting. In fact, great copywriting has a lot to do with their success.

And yes...this means you should have very strong copy too, if you want to get to the top of your game...whatever that game might be.

"But," you might say..."good copywriting is so expensive!"

Yes it is. And bad copywriting is even more expensive.

The simple fact is...if you want to transform your business and become a dominant force in your niche, you will need the absolute *best* copy that money can buy.

If yours is a sizable business, you may already have a budget for copywriting.

But if you don't—and many readers of this book will be small businesses and individuals—then you'll want some tips on what to do and where to go for good copy.

What to Do and Where to Go for Good Copy

The best thing you can *do* is learn copywriting. It's not hard…you could learn the basics of getting leads and sales via the written (or scripted) word in just 12 weeks.

When you learn direct response copywriting, you can accelerate the speed of your business (no more waiting on the copywriter), make faster decisions, know good (and bad) copy when you see it, and save thousands each year.

Being able to write direct response copy empowers you. When I discovered direct response copywriting, I distinctly remember my first thought:

Oh my God! If I learn how to get leads and sales, I'll never be out of work!

Of all of the things you can invest in, gaining the skill of copywriting has got to be one of the most important. Authors routinely win or lose on their book titles; coaches fill their courses (or not) on the strength of their landing pages; entrepreneurs struggle to pay their rent—or enjoy taking the yacht out for a day sail—at least in part, based on the quality of their copy.

There are many copywriting courses available, but I'm going to plug mine. I believe my copywriting course is superior to all others because in my course, the assignments are "real world." You write copy that you will use in your business to gain credibility and to gain leads and sales. In short, my course lets you "earn while you learn."

"But I Can't Write!"

Of course, some business owners will not have the desire (or time) to learn copywriting, or they may be hopeless as a writer no matter how good the teacher. What then?

Well, the obvious option is to go mainstream and seek out a copywriter who fits your niche. That's easy enough, using the appropriate keywords. The more experienced they are, the more they'll be able to help you with marketing and strategy.

If your needs are simple, however, don't be afraid of hiring a "newish" (less costly) copywriter who shows talent in their own website. Today's copywriters have easy access to coaches and mentors who can help them give you the strong work you need—at no extra cost to you.

And finally, avoid Elance® and other bidding sites. This is where very new copywriters go, who are getting paid peanuts for "content."

You don't want content (well, maybe you do). But we're talking about making a big shift in the impact of your business on the world. And you can do that only with strong *direct response* copy.

Sell a System

What do people want?

They want a concrete, step-by-step, "hold my hand" solution.

I've learned this lesson well since 2003, when I developed my first coaching program.

I didn't just wake up one day and say, "Hmmm…I think I'll create a simple step-by-step, 'hold my hand' client acquisition course for solos." Rather, it developed from listening hard to what my coaching students were saying.

Before long, I had the copywriting industry's most powerful marketing system in place. It's been more than a decade and no one has come out with a competing program.

Well, let me rephrase. I have plenty of competition in coaches (including some of my former students).

But to differentiate themselves from me, they say, "*I* don't make you follow a formula. *I'm* more 'free flow.'"

Problem is, unless they're doing therapy or some form of "inner life" coaching, most clients want a plan that gets them to their goal in the shortest possible amount of time. Very few business builders want 100 percent "free flow" coaching.

Yes, it takes a lot of work to create a System. But when you've got a successful System—and your competition doesn't—they're not likely to develop a system of their own. This leaves you in the permanent position of "market leader."

Systems Cement Your Positioning and Help You Become Prominent in Your Niche

In my coaching, I've learned that people want to feel like they're getting a good value for their money. And structure provides that.

After all, in school your teachers didn't say, "Hey, come to class and we'll just wing it…maybe do a little stream of consciousness."

In college, you didn't pay thousands for a "non-agenda" or missing syllabus. No...the learning was intense and "finals" had a reputation.

Bottom line: create a System. Systems are efficient and repeatable. And because they're efficient, they allow you to maximize your time. By building a System that lets you work with groups rather than purely one-on-one, you can reach far more people and change far more lives.

Plus you can charge *more* for a System...and it can last decades.

Get There First (And Do It Better)

If you hang with the Internet marketers for very long, you'll hear the fantastic stories of "KA-CHING" campaigns that had cash coming into the inbox faster that you can say "instant millionaire."

Some of these stories are true, some are embellished, and others have vital missing information...like the 90 percent return rate that sucks the money right back out of the inbox almost as fast as it got there.

I've had my own "instant riches" moments and I'm sure I'll have more. My secret for enjoying financial windfalls is to simply *be aware*.

The First Mover Advantage

The concept of "First Mover Advantage" has been around for decades. Henry Ford and Coca-Cola® are well-known First Mover success stories. But when you experience the power of First Mover Advantage in your own life, the phrase takes on a whole new meaning.

Back in 1998, after getting the boot from the direct response agency I'd worked at for eight years, I put up a website.

Nothing remarkable about that…except that there were only two or three copywriters with websites at that time. For years I did not have to market my business because it took a long time for other copywriters to become *aware* of the Internet opportunity. The Internet delivered clients to me on a silver platter. That was my first experience with the benefits of First Mover Advantage.

Then, in 2003, I decided to coach copywriters. I'd become *aware* of the power of coaching while working with the late John Finn, "talent connector" for some of the world's leading direct response companies. He'd hired a coach to transform his business. And when I saw the result, I had a flash of inspiration.

There were no coaches for copywriters. With all my experience, I could show them the way!

Because I became *aware* of a "hole" in one small but very defined niche—one that I matched to perfectly—I enjoyed First Mover Advantage as a copywriter's coach. Other copywriters tried to discover my secrets, but I wouldn't tell.

During the early years of coaching, I looked for my next First Mover Advantage opportunity. I found it in the creation of the Marlow Marketing Method™ program. I created a System that to this day still ensures a full coaching schedule, with Certified Marlow Marketing Method coaches helping me with the overflow.

And then came the KA-CHING moment. Money flowing into my inbox at the rate of SPAM (faster, actually)…each and every email making me $125 richer.

To reference an earlier teaching in this chapter, this windfall was connected to the True Empathy I had for my marketplace. I knew the deepest pains and greatest frustrations of copywriters and I set out to solve them.

Getting clients was their biggest problem (already solved with my Marlow Marketing Method program). Their next biggest pain was pricing their work. I conducted a survey, did the analysis, and published the 2005 Copywriters Fee & Compensation Survey™.

When I took it to market, I knew it would sell…but I was totally unprepared for the response. Not only was this—once again—the result of being *aware*, but in 2007 and 2014, I published additional volumes, making this very profitable idea a First Mover Advantage three times over.

Was this the end for my string of First Mover Advantages? Not at all. But it's enough to make the point that opportunities are everywhere, if you develop your sense of awareness.

When you're the first to create a solution to a problem in your industry, it automatically makes you a dominant force in your niche, and that opens the floodgates to even more opportunities, and greater financial rewards.

And when you seize the opportunity and create the *best* solution, you ensure that you stay at the top of your niche…and in a position to reap substantial, ongoing rewards.

The Promise of Niche Domination

When you think of success, do you think in terms of incremental advances?

If so, it's okay if you do. Remember the Timothy Ferriss quote that…

> *"The fishing is best where the fewest go, and the collective insecurity of the world makes it easy for people to hit home runs while everyone else is aiming for base hits. There is just less competition for bigger goals."*

So you can dominate your niche with a series of small, incremental steps…or you can hit it big with a quantum leap. It's up to you…but in the end, you wind up at the same place. The only difference *might* be the time it takes you to get there.

Remember that it's your ethical duty to share your gifts…and that the more lives you help change, the greater the good, and the bigger the benefit for both you *and* the people whose lives you touch.

Match yourself with a niche that mirrors *you*, and you'll find your work not only easier and more rewarding…but far more profitable.

Empower yourself and learn copywriting if you can. It's the "secret sauce" of successful entrepreneurs.

And develop and sell a System. Systems are the tools of market leaders.

Finally, develop awareness. Awareness lets you see opportunities that others miss.

Awareness helps you to…

Become a Dominant Force In Your Niche!

Chris Marlow

Websites: http://chrismarlow.com and http://thecopywriterscoach.com

Phone: 760-340-2045

Facebook: www.facebook.com/queenofnichedomination

Twitter: www.twitter.com/Chris_Marlow

LinkedIn: www.linkedin.com/in/christinemarlow

Damiani Sekoulidis

Like you, Damiani couldn't pronounce her name as a child and avoided it altogether until the age of 23. English was among her weakest subjects in high school, so she went on to major in it. Before turning 30, Damiani retired from teaching and bought a one-way ticket to India in pursuit of her doppelgänger. Apparently, she has one in every country. In Thailand she was accidentally nicknamed "Yummy". It stuck. Over the next 13 years, Damiani embarked on a career as a Modern Day Renaissance Woman working in advertising, business administration, modeling, and acting but the gig she's proudest of to date is midwifing her best friend's daughter. Damiani speaks four languages and good spelling makes her swoon. Often dancing in the Mystery, she's a Seeker with superpowers for finding the silver lining in any situation. Embodying the teachings of David Deida, Mama Gena, Dr. John Gray, and Abraham, Damiani admits to being a workshop junkie. A devotee of all things fun with a regular practice in laughter, she loves to dress in costume, gives the best belly hugs, and hates chocolate mousse. Today Damiani can be found inspiring and guiding women to live in their sweet spot.

An Open Letter to Western Women

By Damiani Sekoulidis

Dear Sisters,

I am about to share something that is very personal and close to my heart. Revealing parts of this make me uneasy, but I know the message is important. This is the story of what a girl, on an illuminating journey of pain and pleasure, learns about being a woman. Here goes…

I made my first television appearance at age 10 on a local children's talent show as part of a folk dancing troupe. While excited, I recall also deeply fretting the moment when the host would ask me his classic question, "What do you want to be when you grow up?" I had no clue and asked for my mother's input. As anticipated, before the live audience, he popped that dreaded question to which I impressed him with a wise-beyond-my-years reply, "To be happy."

And that borrowed answer has deeply informed my life choices. After all, if mum thought it was a worthy goal, then it really had to be. And yet herein lies the irony—how often do we give advice but rarely heed our own. So bless my well-meaning mother for imparting such great wisdom to me, yet not having the means to embody it herself.

> *"Some of my most important teachers in life have been the people who showed me how NOT to be."* ~ Jean Haner

Like Mother Like Daughter

I can't remember the exact age I decided I wasn't going to be like my mother. I'm not even sure it was a conscious decision. But I wasn't inspired by the life I saw her...enduring. An unhappy marriage she didn't have the courage to leave because she didn't know the value of her happiness. (Saying this makes me uncomfortable, as if I'm betraying her somehow.) I understand it's all she knew. She did the best she could with what was passed down to her. Which reminds me of something I once read from Dr. Christiane Northrup about the deep bond between mothers and daughters that had a way of creating an unconscious agreement to carry on the family lineage of stoic suffering. But my mother's sacrificial path didn't feel right to me. I knew there had to be more to life. More than staying married "for the sake of the kids," putting everyone else's needs first, swallowing disappointment, settling, seeking fulfillment by bearing and caring for children, ignoring the body's warnings, denying personal needs and joy. There just had to be a better way. Thank Goddess for the fierce, greedy, and wild part of me that knew better and insisted on having more. Having fun. Exploring. Breaking rules. Coming first.

> *"To become optimally healthy and happy, each of us must get clear about the ways in which our mother's history both influenced and continues to inform our state of health, our beliefs, and how we live our lives. Every woman who heals herself helps heal all the women who came before her and all those who will come after her." ~ Dr. Christiane Northrup*

It's My Pleasure

The main reason I struggled as a child with that "What-do-you-want-to-be" question was because I simply wanted to do nothing in life other than PLAY. But shocking as it may be, getting paid to do so wasn't among the viable career options presented to me growing up. Nor was it the kind of lifestyle modeled by my mother. So what's a girl to do? I admit, for a while I pretzeled myself trying to follow the rules in the Game of Life. But there was no fooling my wise body. And after years of ignoring many painful signs and witnessing other women, especially my mother, also suffer physically, I finally drew a line in the sandbox. I chose to reclaim my feminine aliveness and pledge allegiance to my old playful friend. This time as a woman it meant embracing pleasure as a priority.

As my reverence for pleasure deepened, I would get even more frustrated with my martyr mother for over-giving, caring for everyone else but herself, tolerating men, alone pushing through 12-hour days, 6 days/week in her business and skipping breaks because her customers "needed her"…you get it. But now I realize why she did. She was acting out something biologically universal to all women. Something critical for us to understand which I'll explain in a bit.

But for now, you and I both know this is not an isolated incident. You can see yourself and/or someone you know playing out parts of the same story. And I am writing you with a sincere plea to stop this madness. We simply cannot go on this way. Not only can we not afford to keep it up personally, but our families, businesses, and communities will suffer. They need us. They so desperately need us at our best. You heard the Dalai Lama say, "The world will be saved by the western woman." But not if we don't save ourselves first.

Sadly, it's too late for my sweet mama. Today at the young age of 63, she can no longer drive, cook, use the telephone, zip up her coat, put on her seatbelt, talk clearly, live without medication, or remember what she ate for lunch 5 minutes ago. It breaks my heart and yet I am grateful for her example. Since I intuitively sensed all along what is now being confirmed scientifically, I believe her decline into dementia was avoidable.

Woes of the Western Woman

As you know, times have changed. Yes, so many more opportunities are available to us now that weren't for our mothers or our mother's mothers (hallelujah to social change!), but we are approaching this new bounty in a way that doesn't account for the unique biochemical makeup of our gorgeous female form. Look around. Our culture is rewarding women to be more like men—do more, focus, compete, keep up, get ahead, produce. And at the same time, we're still moonlighting as women with the same ol' responsibilities. But it's not working for us. Our bodies aren't designed to take it the way it's being dished out. It's simply not sustainable. According to psychologist and *New York Times* best-selling author Dr. John Gray, PhD, studies have shown that due to our unique physiology (our hormones, brain/body wiring, blood flow to the limbic system), women carry, on average, twice the amount of stress that men do in the workplace. Get her home and her stress levels double. Um...you don't have to be a mathematician to know that that adds up to no good.

Look, it's no accident that today's women are dealing with epidemic levels of heart disease, depression, anxiety, eating disorders, breast cancer, self-loathing, dwindling sex drives, and get this...decreasing life expectancy. That's right, we're now living shorter lives. With psychology studies reporting women's happiness rates at an all-time low, having now slipped below that of men's, so many women have become the walking dead. Slogging from one responsibility to another to the next and to yet one more, without properly countering the negative effects of juggling so many more balls. Because women are nurturers by nature, we tend to put others first and many don't even know how to self-care (like my beloved mother). It's not something that's been taught or encouraged and so many struggle to even give themselves permission to ease up. After all, there's no time…the job depends on it…the guilt…no one else will do it…it's selfish...the children will starve. Yet we can't put our needs off anymore—the statistics are staggering.

> *"The American Psychological Association research study 'Stress in America,' reports that women are more fearful about the current financial situation than men. Women are reporting more physical and psychological symptoms, including sleep disturbance, headaches, mood swings and changes in appetite. In fact, more than one-third of women currently rank their stress level as 'extreme'."*

In a recent issue of *O Magazine*, Dr. Oz claims every woman must ask herself this question right now: **"Am I managing my stress?** *The fact that stress is bad for your health is no surprise, but a recent study found that women who experienced a greater number of stressors (work problems, divorce, family illness) in middle age were more likely to develop dementia. Chronic stress may trigger the production of inflammatory compounds and damage areas of the brain linked to memory."* Sound familiar?

There are no two ways about it: in order to support our fulfillment, vitality, and longevity in this faster-paced new world, we must learn how to effectively manage modern day stress. Like women.

> *"A woman's greatest challenge in learning to cope more effectively with stress is to begin caring for herself as much as she is caring for others."* – Dr. John Gray, PhD

Did you hear that? We've got to put on the oxygen mask first before helping our neighbor. We need a full cup in order to generously share with the next person. We must fill our tank with the proper feminine fuel to decrease the stress that's a result of living in a masculine world.

The (Other) Big O

Along the way, I've learnt that a way of saying YES to ourselves as women is by committing to self-care—with pleasure as our superfood. After all, the way women fuel up is by stimulating The Big O. Say what? Well, the Other Big O. Here's the thing gals: our entire system is reliant on the love hormone Oxytocin. It's what makes us feel good. Oxytocin is the hormone that promotes bonding in both sexes, yet reduces stress in women (testosterone does it for men). Without sufficient amounts of Oxytocin, try as we may, we simply cannot lower our stress levels. And here's a gentle reminder, in different words, of the cost of chronic stress: no energy, dissatisfaction, lack of feeling love, cranky panties, creativity missing-in-action, illness, disease, inability to enjoy pleasure or sensuality or…uh…orgasm. Yep, Oxytocin regulates sexual response and allows climax. Got your attention now? Stimulate your "Big O" by participating in activities that involve sharing, caring, befriending, and nurturing. In the "good ol' days" our lifestyle naturally produced Oxytocin. The pace was slower, we worked among other women, we were in constant company—it was easy to create the hormones that supported our well-being. But our current fast-paced, corporate-chick-supermom lifestyles are literally killing us: on a physical and soul level. It's time to develop a daily self-care practice to boost Oxytocin production to counter the stress of our speedy, get-it-done culture.

But there's a glitch…rebuilding or stimulating Oxytocin alone doesn't reduce stress. What does is actually using up the Oxytocin. We instinctively do this by nurturing others and giving unconditionally. Uh…is this a trick? Nope. The kicker is that women's brains, unlike men's, are designed with a built-in reward system that says, "If I nurture others, then my stress goes down and I feel awesome." However, there's a danger of overextending ourselves, as we need healthy levels of Oxytocin before we can nurture the tribe. No wonder women find it so hard to say 'no' and 'receiving' is among the greatest challenges today. Because when a woman is stressed, she wants to give.

This brings me back to that point about now understanding why my mother was spreading herself so thin. She had tripped that wire—her system was merely trying to cope with the madness of being a wife + mother + business owner. Her brain was telling her to give and give and give in a desperate attempt to use up Oxytocin and reduce her stress. The problem: her tank was already dry.

> *"When a woman is not getting what she needs, she feels an urge to give more...unless she learns to put on the brakes, she can easily run herself into the ground." – Dr. John Gray, PhD*

Now, if you're a man crashing this party and can't see how this relates to you, IT DOES. You likely know a woman or two, right? You may even have one of your own. And I know what a turn-on it is for you to see your lady happy, alive, juicy, and in her pleasure. Not just for the O-bvious reasons but because when she is embodying her feminine side, she's more in touch with her appreciation for you, which in turn reduces YOUR stress. So help her get there (and take the credit)! But you can only top her off—the majority of the work is her responsibility. Encourage her to recharge her batteries regularly by taking time for herself, doing things she loves, investing in what fulfills her and getting the emotional support she needs by spending time with other women. Do yourselves both this favor, because women are inherently generous so when Mama's happy, EVERYONE'S happy!

Get Happy with these "Big O" Stimulators:

- **SPACIOUS SCHEDULE.** Sloooow down. Seriously, the number one greatest inhibitor of Oxytocin in women is being rushed. (This is also the case in the bedroom, gentlemen.) Just think about it: your husband is waiting by the door urging you to hurry up or you're trying to pack the kids into the car as they are running late for school or you slept in and have to run to a meeting or you have a date and only 20 minutes to get ready...You stressed out yet? Nothing inspires in me a bigger sigh of calm than being relieved of a tight squeeze on time. How does your body react to the thought of having a jam-packed morning of go-go-go and all of a sudden having your afternoon open up? Ahhh, right?

- **SACRED SELF-CARE.** Partaking in what you love, pleasure, massages, pampering, time outs, a bath, naptime, walks on the beach, a cup of tea, girlfriend getaways, saying "no"...just give yourself permission to indulge in self-nurturing daily. Your health truly depends on it.

> "Rest and self-care are so important. When you take time to replenish your spirit, it allows you to serve others from the overflow. You cannot serve from an empty vessel." ~ Eleanor Brownn

- **DEEP BREATHING.** With breath being the source of life, this should be no surprise. Deep breathing is the quickest, least expensive, and most effective way to relax your system. Close your eyes...in through the nose, out through the mouth. (Yoga works too.)

- **REACH OUT AND TOUCH SOMEONE.** Too many women these days are touch-starved, especially if single or without small cuddly children. Whether with a lover, friend, parent, child or pet, get your canoodle on. Hugs have been shown to benefit blood pressure, reduce cortisol (stress hormone) levels, and when you hold it for 20 seconds or longer, it releases Oxytocin.

"We need four hugs a day for survival. We need eight hugs a day for maintenance. We need twelve hugs a day for growth." ~ Virginia Satir

WASH YOUR MOUTH OUT WITH SOAP. Language matters and affects Oxytocin. Practice positive self-talk and when it comes to going over your "To Do" list, just notice the difference in your body when you move from saying, "I have to…I need to…" TO "I get to…I choose to…I desire to…" Yes?

- **COMMUNITY.** Spending time connecting with like-hearted people, expressing emotions, sharing desires, feeling seen + heard + acknowledged + supported, knowing you're not alone…it'll carry you to beautiful places.

- **GIRLS' NIGHT OUT.** Or in, it doesn't really matter. Just women spending time together has been proven to combat depression. Gather with your gals, join a women's group, take a class…just find your sisters and sit together. Often.

- **ROMANCE.** Receiving compliments, flowers, touch, going on dates, feeling loved, experiencing pleasure…all of these goodies can be enjoyed on your own too—so no excuses. And do it regularly!

- **SINGING & DANCING.** The uninhibited expression of self-releases your sensual Shakti power, increases energy, reduces depression, and creates new neural pathways. Whether on your own or in front of others, just let 'er rip!

"Learning tango or singing in public are important pleasurable pursuits. We're taught that good women spend their free time endlessly giving, selflessly serving and never caring about themselves. Dancing is all about me, being in my body and feeling pleasure, it gives others permission to indulge in their own gratification. Joy starts in our bodies, as nitric oxide and neurotransmitters, and then its positive energy heals our cells and then radiates outward to heal others and the planet. Dancing is a form of healing—in fact, any ecstatic experience can be healing not just for you but for others. We have to be joyful, dance, and bring pleasure into our lives deliberately." – Dr. Christiane Northrup

- **ANTICIPATION.** The mere anticipation of doing anything you love (i.e., expecting romance, experiencing pleasure, basking in self-care) stimulates Oxytocin production. A classic example is looking forward to a vacation. You're not even there yet, with weeks to go and yet you're already buzzing in anticipation. So schedule that spa day, girls' night and dinner date into your calendar, keep referring to your agenda book, and ride the high.

Bringing it Home

Though it's been a bittersweet journey, my mother's life is a precious gift to me. My biggest wakeup call. Because of her, I learned to honor my truth. Because of her, I value, even more, the necessity of embracing my pleasure and desires. As a result, today I stand for all women living deeply inspired and pleasurable lives. Though I can still choke on tradition (feeling shackled by responsibility and putting off fun), I always find my way back. It's too important not to—joy, in all its forms, is not a frivolous luxury, but our lifeline. As fully embodied and alive women, we have such potent gifts to share. The world needs the juice of our light, compassion, ecstasy, feminine power and divine wisdom. Please sisters, walk with me on this radical self-loving path. Make your pleasure a priority. For you. For my mother. For all women. Thank you.

To Contact Damiani:

Website: www.thepleasurepriestess.com

Facebook: www.facebook.com/liveinyoursweetspot

Cheryl Ginnings

Cheryl Ginnings has been married to Monte Ginnings almost 49 years. They have three children and five grandchildren. Their oldest, Blake, has cerebral palsy and has been an inspiration to the family and to those who know him.

Although Cheryl was a full-time mom at home with the children growing up, she finished her degree at Sam Houston State University in 1992 with honors dealing with families with special needs children. She produced a video about this that was used on TV and at two universities.

When the youngest was ready to attend college, Cheryl had to begin working and decided on real estate. She excelled in this and won lots of awards and honors for her work with others. She was in the first Leadership OAR class of 2005.

During their years as a minister's family, Cheryl was active in helping others in every way possible. She started a network for minister's wives and later to help others connect when they are experiencing problems.

During the past year, Cheryl was a co-author of a book that became an International Best-selling book compiled by Anita Sechesky

Cheryl offers insight into everyday challenges and helps people realize they are not alone. She loves speaking and writing.

REPURPOSED, NOT reTIRED!

By Cheryl Ginnings

I love to hear the story about how eagles love their eaglets, but still know that eaglets have to learn to fly. It must be difficult for the mother eagle to prepare her nest with thorns around the edges to get ready to send her babies out of the nest, but it has to be done for the babies to learn what God made them to do—FLY!

When the time comes, the mother eagle gently nudges the babies to the edge of the nest and pushes the baby until they are uncomfortable enough that they basically fall out of the nest. The babies, not knowing what happened, flap their wings in an attempt to stop whatever is happening to them. This does not work, but they are falling fast while the mother is watching close by. At just the right time, the mother eagle swoops under the baby and lets the eaglet ride on her back up to the nest, only to do this over and over. This happens until the baby eaglet can fly on its own! Exciting!

It reminds me of when I was a little girl and my father came home one day and asked me if I would give my tricycle to my younger sister. I was sad and did not want to, but I knew he would not ask me to do something I should not do. Reluctantly, I agreed that she could have my trike! Then he turned around and opened the car door and pulled out a new bike without training wheels.

You can imagine how my sadness turned into joy as I saw a new bike and wanted to ride it immediately! I would pedal a couple of times and fall over. I did this over and over until I was in tears. I wanted to ride, but I could not do it the first try!

My father encouraged me to keep trying and told me that I could do it without going through the time of training wheels. I wanted to, but I did not think I could! It was hard to try and fall over and scrape my knees! But sure enough, by the end of the day, I was riding like a champ! I did it!!! I was excited to ride alone!

Life is like that in several ways. Challenges come to us that we do not believe we can handle. It is an opportunity that sounds great, but there is so much self-doubt! It is hard to think of being able to do things that are not in our comfort zones. When another person just says that they believe in us, it gives strength to try until we achieve dreams that were once thought impossible.

When I was first married many years ago, my husband came home and told me that someone needed me to teach a class of Bible schoolteachers how to teach children. I immediately told him, "I can't do that!" He assured me I could and that I just had to be prepared.

Again, I retold him that I could not take on doing such a task, and he would not let me out of this challenge. He reminded me that if I prepared myself, I could do it. He was so right. He saw in me something I did not see in myself.

Later on, he asked me to teach a ladies' Bible class. I was younger by far than those in the class and I said I could not do it. The ladies in the class would know more than I did, and they should teach. He did not let it go! He told me again that I could do it! He said that if I would study well, I would know more than others did on any subject. He again saw in me the ability to do something I did not see in myself.

There are times in everyone's life that other people can look on and see things that should be developed in another person with a talent they need to develop. Teachers have students in their classes who need to be encouraged to reach out and grow with their personal talents. It may only take a little time to tell someone what is possible. Just a word or two of encouragement can change lives! Encouragement can instill confidence in another to do great things in life!

I attended a workshop just a year ago where I was taught to set goals by stating them in the present tense as if it had already been achieved. Each sentence began with, "I AM." As I wrote my goals in the present tense, it came to me there were many things I wanted to do. Goal setting was never easy for me. Many efforts were just in the form of a wish. Previous goals could not be measured or even attained, so they were just wishes.

This method of stating them was different. As I wrote out what I desired to happen in my life, I wrote big things. I wrote them as if it was already done and I was successful! Then as the moderator asked for a volunteer to read their statements out loud in front of the audience, I was aware that my hand was in the air quickly. Immediately, a microphone appeared as I was asked to read them slowly out loud.

There I stood in front of almost 3,000 people I did not know as I began to read the statements aloud. There was a hush over the audience. I began with, "I AM an international author. I AM an international speaker..." When I finished, the director of the program just said, "Wow. Did you hear the power in the statements?" That was so incredible for me to stand and state out loud what I hoped to do and be!

The power was in writing the statements as if the goals had happened and in stating them out loud. Letting others know what you want to accomplish seems to keep you focused and strong. The whole weekend, many people came up to me congratulating me on what I said and encouraging me by saying they knew I would reach my goals!

Some even met me with tears in their eyes saying they were so touched with my statements. Since they were personal statements, it was surprising that there was that kind of reaction in the audience. But the truth is, I was stronger from that day and more focused on reaching those goals. I read about thirty things I wanted to do. The achievements I have reached are amazing! It has been less than a year and I can say, "I am an international best-selling author!" What pleasure it is to say that.

Before you read this chapter, I will have spoken out of the country. I will be an International Speaker! The power of setting goals like this is amazing!

The subconscious mind accepts what we say as true. If we focus on negative things and tell ourselves that we are unable to do things, well, we are right!!! If we are putting ourselves down and stating how inadequate we feel, or how ugly we are, or how unable we are to do something, it becomes true! We become that way!

When we simply state things in a positive way and say how capable we are, that can also become true! From now on, I plan to state my goals as if they are already true and they are positive and uplifting! Why choose to be a negative person incapable of change, if just changing our minds and what we say to ourselves changes reality?

The world is full of negative people, so be a positive influence wherever you are. Speak positive words of encouragement to others often. Look for the good in others and then help share the good things you see they are capable of doing! They might surprise themselves with wonderful changes.

I want to give you another example of this kind of encouragement. My niece has some kind of developmental issue that has never been diagnosed. She was able to do lots of schoolwork in a slower way, but athletically, she loved sports. Her mom and dad encouraged her in golf, snow skiing, horseback riding, and doing things to keep her body in shape.

While she was in the seventh grade, her physical education teacher saw her one day with some girls and asked her if she wanted to come and run with the other girls in her class. She was so excited about being asked to join the other girls and she began to run with the girls every day. Long story short, she became quite good at running. She could run long distance.

A few years ago, the Special Olympics were held in Athens, Greece, and my niece was in attendance to represent the state of Idaho. She was great at running and even though she was sick with a stomach bug, she ran and took home a medal!

My point in telling you this is that sometimes we overlook others we assume will not be able to do things and, therefore, we do not take the effort to get to know them and encourage them to try new things.

Setting goals can be tricky. There are some things we cannot change. There is no need to say I want to be taller, because as I grow older, I am getting shorter. That is not fun. I wish I could be taller, but I do not need to set that as a goal. It won't happen.

Goals have to be attainable. In fact, a goal has to be measurable to know if you are on track. What would happen if we set goals and never started to work on reaching them? It goes without saying that to set a goal is to begin to prepare for it. Start with taking classes or learn how to improve your skills at the things you want to succeed in doing. There are so many classes online that can improve many skills. What is it that you want to improve? What do you want to achieve?

So many people have the idea that they cannot achieve something they desire. A person in authority may have told them negative things. Our son has cerebral palsy and we, as his parents, were told several times that he would never amount to anything and that we should put him away and forget he was born.

After moving across country for a special school, one specialist told us that he would even try to keep him out of that school. It was absolutely unbelievable! It still is hard to think that someone would have the guts to say that anyone could never improve with some help! Even if that was a thought, what harm does it do to try to get some help to see if improvements could be possible?

The good thing is that the other five on the panel gave him an opportunity to learn. Without specialists helping us to understand what was wrong and how he learned differently from us, we would have never known how to help our own son.

The wonderful thing that happened was that we had an opportunity to learn how to watch for things he could change and learn to accept what could not be changed. However, with different doctors and at a different time in life, more growth might have taken place. Educationally, all have discovered how special people learn in ways that are not normally used in public education or in therapists' training.

Our son later became an artist from a therapist who used the small movements using one hand stretching his long-range motions to paint abstract art. Those who loved his work bought many of his pictures. He decorated fourteen Southern Dental Clinics in the Houston area years ago. He was recognized as a special artist by Texas A&M. He has a painting in Seattle at the University of

Washington's Medical School. Others have bought paintings and enjoy them in their homes and offices.

In 2000, our son's art was on display at a museum. In one month, he sold forty paintings. He would not have been able to do anything if we had listened to specialists early on and decided that he could not succeed. But we did not! We believed that we could teach him things! He did learn a lot! He did not learn everything, but none of us do.

Our son has so much love and shares that with everyone who is nice to him. He is easy to love. It is a blessing to have a special person in our lives who teaches us to be patient and loving to all people. He is still growing in his ability to communicate and show his likes and dislikes with others. What if we had believed the doctor who told us to put him away and forget we had him?

Why would I tell you all these stories? To share with you that everyone needs to have goals. Sometimes there are people in our lives who need help setting goals and just like my husband encouraged me to teach and speak in front of groups, we have been able to help our son to grow. It has been a pleasure to share ways that we tried to help him learn to walk and ride a trike and anything we thought there was a possibility he could learn. Many things did not work. But we never gave up on trying to find new ways to teach him.

If you are stuck in life and don't know what you want to do, find someone who can help you see what talents you might have hidden. Ask for help to set some goals for yourself. Always state them in the present tense and in a way that shows you have already achieved it. Use "I AM" statements to describe your next steps.

After you write them out, post them where you will not forget what you set out to accomplish. Your mind is easily distracted and getting off track is easy to do. Success is just starting over to keep on track.

The eagles learn to fly because the mom knows that it will be hard and it will take them several tries to make it possible, but their moms don't give up. They build the nest in a way that makes it uncomfortable to stay "at home." Some parents could learn a lesson from eagles and make things uncomfortable for their kids to move out and be on their own. There are young people who are able to work and support themselves, but feel it is more comfortable to stay at home because mom and dad take care of them.

How long do you think it takes to develop Olympic athletes? Probably, each champion would say a lifetime. They have to dream an impossible dream and practice until they hurt all over and push some more. They may practice their skills until their hands or feet are bleeding, but that does not stop them. They have a dream and will not give up because it takes work! Lots of work!! Never give up!

Life is a challenge for all, but growth does not take place when we stay in our comfort-zones. Growth is meant to be a challenge. School subjects were harder for us a little at a time. We did not go from addition to calculus, but one step at a time. Our goals must be achievable.

When our girls were ready to go to college, my husband and I wanted them to attend Christian colleges, but as a minister's family, we did not have the money to send them. I had to find a job to help pay this. Not knowing if I would succeed, I began as a Realtor, but soon excelled and got leadership awards.

Last year as my husband was retiring, I knew I wanted to be an international author and international speaker. I worked on classes, listened to tapes, started joining groups to network with others and volunteer to speak to any group that I could.

One by one, doors opened for me. It was a difficult year for us personally and financially, but I had dreams of what I wanted to accomplish. I want to write more and speak more. Every time I take advantage of one opportunity, another seems to come. It is a wonderful feeling to know that I prepared myself to take on more challenges as I grow older. I knew that my husband would be stepping down from full-time ministry and after forty-five years of working, there was still more on our wish list to accomplish.

Our lives have been "repurposed, not reTIRED"! Many people do not live long after if they retire and sit down. Life needs purpose! Life is meant for living! We have repurposed our lives to be full of things to accomplish! Why stop when we can keep doing more and different things than we did most of our lives?

REPURPOSE your life at any age to be more! Repurpose to set goals for things you have never done before. Learn new skills! Learn how to improve your health, your wealth, or whatever you desire. Your life is in your control. You cannot change others, but you can change yourself!

Believe it is possible to achieve your dreams! Keep them posted in the present tense and don't get discouraged if you do not succeed the first time you try something new. Eagles did not learn to fly the first time. I did not learn to ride my bicycle the first time, but I did the first day! Never give up! Never quit!

Cheryl Ginnings

International Author and Speaker

Consultant

Broker, Realtor, CRS

Manager of Send Out Cards

5005 NW Meadowbrook DR.

Lawton, OK 73505 and starting

Phone: (580) 591-6868

FB: Cheryl.ginnings author

Twitter: cherylginnings

LinkedIn: Cheryl Ginnings

Websites: www.cherylginnings.com and www.speakercheryl.com

Deborah Crowe

"She is clothed with strength and dignity, and she laughs without fear of the future." –Proverbs 31:25

Deborah Crowe is a natural-born thought leader. Her clients have welcomed her coaching with high energy, a great sense of humor, mentorship, positive attitude, and the ability to never see barriers, only opportunity. She brings out the best in all of her clients with integrity and true authenticity.

Deborah has been referred to as a Master Teacher and mentor to men and women of all ages. She has been a coach, author, educator, and professional speaker since 1990.

As a Work Life Balance Specialist, Deborah supports men and women who have placed themselves on the backburner in life. She boosts them emotionally and gives them the tools to manage employment, family, and self so that they can regain their Work Life Balance. It's not about strategy; it's about a new way of thinking.

Deborah brings a level of grit as an entrepreneur like no other. She is extremely resilient and has demonstrated this ability in her own life. Setting constant goals and being a lifelong learner is her daily mantra.

Deborah is located in Canada and has expanded her clientele to national and international clients working via telephone and Skype. The first session with Deborah is complimentary to establish a connection, rapport, and develop a plan of action.

If you are in a position where it's time to make that decision for a change in your life, whether it is a relationship, new career, or just a simple change to embrace Work Life Balance, Deborah can assist you.

"Work Life Balance is not a trend; it's a lifestyle." –Mama Deb

Work–Life Balance Seen through the Eyes of a Renaissance Woman

By Deborah Crowe

"With the new day comes strength and new thought."—Eleanor Roosevelt

Do you like the choices you are making at home and at work?

Work. Life. Balance. Three simple words—yet many people struggle to understand the meaning of this achievable life.

Work–life balance is not a trend. It's a decision—coupled with time management skills—which equates to a lifestyle of meaning, both in your career and your personal life.

Life is not meant to be lived with perfectly outlined schedules on a day-to-day basis. Emergencies happen. Life happens. The key is to make a decision on how to respond to these bumps along life's highway and, in a more important way, get yourself back on track.

Society has put us into a warped speed for everything as a result of schedules at work and at home to ensure that our children are stimulated before and after school with so many activities. It's no wonder that drive-through restaurants were created, and now we have a huge problem with obesity in North America.

There is no set equation to determine how to live with work–life balance. It boils down to one element: acceptance. Your lifestyle dictates how your personal life and work life will ebb and flow.

Is there a true science to happiness? Many people who have work–life balance and are able to sustain it on a regular basis seem to be very happy and fulfilled. Is there a part of our DNA that already sets the tone for our work–life balance that is altered based on our life experiences?

Like any life change, you have to instill within your own mind a true cognitive shift—a mind-set that cannot be compromised. Everyone on planet Earth has the same amount of time each week—168 hours—to fit in all of their activities of daily living into their schedule.

Time. It's the essence of our being. Schedules, deadlines, expirations—how you choose to spend your months, weeks, minutes, and seconds can be a tumultuous task.

What does your weekly schedule breakdown look like?

Let's take out the hours we know for sure or use a best-guess scenario:

ONE-WEEK SCHEDULE SAMPLE FOR WORK–LIFE BALANCE

Task	Time spent	Scenario/variance
Work	40 hours	Based on a full-time job
Sleep	56 hours	Based on 8 hours per night
Exercise	7 hours	1 hour, 7 days/week
Social	8 hours	Date night 4 hours; networking 4 hours
Self-care	7 hours	Based on 60 minutes/day (morning routine, reading/quiet escape/meditation)
Family	35 hours	Based on 5 hours/day (morning/afternoon/evening combined)
Friends	3 hours	Based on one or two visits
Church	1.5 hours	Based on one Sunday service
Total	157.5 hours	Does this look like your weekly work–life balance equation?

You will note from the table above that the total number of hours is 157.5. Where would you spend the remaining 10.5 hours?

Work–life balance takes patience, practice, and constant assessment to achieve a balance that will work for you. Your scheduling and task list will constantly be changing; however, if you have a plan in place, you are setting the foundation for success.

Each element of work–life balance can change from week to week.

A perfect example of this is work. Your employer may offer you overtime and/or you may have to work on a statutory holiday.

Sleep. Yes, we would all love to have eight hours of beautiful, deep sleep, but most people are walking around on serious sleep deprivation.

Exercise. It's a must. You have to move your body every day and get your heart rate up! It's the best modality for stress reduction—and it helps you sleep!

Social time is very important because it allows you to connect with your friends and just have fun! Laughter is the best medicine, and you must find the time to connect because social time is and can also be an element of your self-care as well!

Family should always come first. With hectic, busy schedules and each family member heading in a different direction, embrace the "preschool" moments and "after-school" time if you have the opportunity to do so. With many families who have both parents working full-time, this makes the dinner hour and evening hours even more special.

There is no schedule or work–life balance equation that is set in stone or is perfect. This is a very personal exercise, which is why I wanted to provide you with a template to use (http://bit.ly/1MqGB2s).

Being open to reviewing, assessing, analyzing, and reorganizing your time is key here. The goal is to ensure that each element of your life is given time each day. It's going to take a few days to modify your schedule and truly implement a new work–life balance. However, if you stick with it for three weeks, a new habit (schedule) will be completed, and you can implement it every day!

Having unbalance in your life is a reflective time for growth, change, and progression. Unbalance allows you to look at the reasons for the chaos, get back on track, and perhaps instill some new rituals into your life.

Many people see failure as a negative. Failure is a huge opportunity that is usually coupled with rejection, but this is the door opening wide for your next success or opportunity. Work–life balance can be disguised in many ways. However, not all opportunities come as a beautifully wrapped package with a red bow delivered to your front door.

Communication is a key factor for work–life balance, both with your family for your personal life and with your employer and/or clients for your work life. Both can be in sync beautifully if the lines of communication flow smoothly, and such synchronization demonstrates that you've intentionally planned and designed your life.

Traveling for work can be a work–life balance factor that tips the scales toward unbalance. You need to find the ten-minute time "zappers" and eliminate them. It's just as important to follow a routine when traveling and not let the beeps and alarms of technology become a work–life balance hack that constantly interrupts you and challenges your attention and concentration.

Many people get stuck and do not know where to start when they become unraveled in a schedule that has them buried. The key is to be creative. Be specific with yourself and create attainable goals. The old cliché "less is better" works well in this development because you are creating mini-milestones, not running a marathon of events within your schedule. Mini-milestones turn into huge accomplishments and finished tasks and projects. Set a goal to do one BIG thing per day and do not waver.

Life changes. You cannot have a "what if" mentality. Is it the right time? You are the only person who can answer that question. What is my best advice? Do it when you are ready.

What is my methodology to make big leaps? Have an action plan. Seek your opportunity and execute it when you know and feel it's the right time and you have decided to own what you have created.

GRIT. I love this word. It's the true meaning of who and what I am. Every entrepreneur has it. It's a cognitive element that is crucial to seeking and sustaining work–life balance.

We all want harmony in our lives because it is how our brains interpret success, which is directly linked to the cognitive-emotional connection of work–life balance. So why do we strive for perfection? What is perfection? Is this a generational recurring belief system? When does life become happy for people? Does work–life balance bring happiness? Success?

People view work–life balance differently because each individual has his or her own core belief system based on his or her childhood experiences, upbringing, parents' beliefs, losses, education, etc. Is there a genetic predisposition? Is it in our DNA? Do we repeat what our parents did, or do we strive to do and be better? Is work–life balance based on materialism, and is this what we base our successes in life on?

Work–life balance is about growth, acceptance, and progression, NOT perfection.

Think about work–life balance with the metaphor of riding a bike—it's all about repetition and your attitude in falling off and then getting back on!

How can you grow without losses and lessons? This is now the growth that you foster and sustain.

Core beliefs that are well-honed create a mastery of lifestyle, which is work–life balance at its best.

Work–life balance develops as you age, and it matures as you experience lifestyle changes and achieve goals and dreams.

Work–life balance is an ongoing re-evaluation of who you are and what you want from your life, both personally and professionally.

Accept change, because life will happen (such as the death of a loved one).

Work–life balance can be one's acceptance of what is. For example, you are swamped at work, your house is a mess, and your child is sick. All of this can throw a curveball and disrupt anyone's work–life balance. The point is to accept the unbalance called life, work through what is important, which is foremost our health and our loved ones. Schedules, deadlines, and commitments will always be there, but sometimes they have to take a backseat.

Being happy is directly linked to having achieved work–life balance. Many people suffer with depression that is related to their personal life or work or, unfortunately, sometimes both, which can be difficult if you do not have a good support system in place.

You have to believe in yourself and know that there are always greater things to come in your life because we are meant to be lifelong learners, challenge ourselves to grow, and jump out of our comfort zones.

Do things that challenge you. The end result is newfound knowledge that you can instill into your daily life. New knowledge is wasted if you don't apply it.

When you change, so does your work–life balance, and it's always evolving with you.

Here are 12 tips that you can start with to re-evaluate your work–life balance:

Schedule the important things

Implement and exercise time management

Communicate with your employer about flex-time

Bring in backup

Communicate with other families

Be mindful of scheduling too many extracurricular activities

Schedule routine, regular family time

Take time for you

Ensure you have "couple" time

Share your work experience with your children

Make time for fun

Don't miss those special moments

Work–life balance does not mean scheduling your child(ren) in every activity to the point that you are running yourself ragged and there is no "me" time.

Looking back on the 1950s to today, it's an interesting dynamic of where we have come from. *Housekeeping Magazine* (May 13, 1955) published "The Good Wife's Guide." It was a well-documented bulleted list of what a good wife should do upon the arrival of her husband from his hard day at the office. The interesting observation is that the wife is beautifully dressed, as if she works in an office, and she is donned with a lovely pressed apron. Her work–life balance skills were that of a facility manager. She ran the home and all of the logistics that come with it—including "always knowing her place."

As the decades passed, working women, who were also wives and mothers, embraced work–life balance. It was like a combination of Betty Crocker, June Cleaver, and Martha Stewart. Now that's an exemplary skill set worth noting for work–life balance at its finest.

Modern-day working moms range from the amazing stay-at-home moms all the way to CEOs of large companies. Their commonality is that they share the same goals, just on different levels. It's a daily struggle for many. However, they all have the well-honed talents of pure and simple acceptance as well as the ability to juggle.

Who is our role model for work–life balance? This is something to really ponder. Do we need to conform to a role model? There is not a single perfect person on the Earth who can "do it all." Sure it can be done with a huge support system in place. But doesn't having a support system really just encompass basic decision-making, logistics, and the mastered skill of delegation?

Stress that is self-inflicted is not going to lead you to work–life balance. Women are extremely hard on themselves and always looking to be that perfect mom or perfect wife. Whose value system are they looking to model this behavior after?

A recent Harvard study (https://hbr.org/2014/11/let-employees-choose-when-where-and-how-to-work) found that adults want freedom. They want both the flexibility and ability to work remotely. Working from a home office brings out innovation and creativity as people work from their own private environments that offer them relaxation and comfort. Such environments increase productivity, but also offer companies retention of valuable employees.

According to the study, "Companies that officially allow employees to work remotely at least three times per month were more likely to report revenue growth of 10% or more within the last year, compared to firms without such policies."

I've spoken to many people, both men and women, about the topic of work–life balance. It's very interesting to hear their individual views of what it means to them. The takeaway of my discussions is that everyone wants to be happy and live a simple life. Perception, judgment, and life scenarios cloud this for many. However, there are people who have chosen to break free from this pattern of behavior and live that powerful life of balance. It was a privilege to speak to men and women all over the world by telephone, email, text message, Skype, and all of the powerful tools that allow us to communicate so effectively today, yet such tools also tip the scale for many and push them into a life unbalanced.

As a mom, it truly saddens me to see parents at events with their children. You probably already get the picture here. The parent's head is down, not watching his or her son or daughter, checking that email, sending that text. There is nothing more important than giving your children time and love. This is a huge problem that I see growing in our society and is a contributing factor to non-work–life balance. What are you teaching your children and the generations to come?

Children today are overexposed to technology. The old days of traditional play seem to be far gone. Our society has become prescription dependent, with enhanced social withdrawal. Where would a child learn work–life balance if people do not model it at home, in the community, and at school, where they spend five to six hours per day for several years? Don't get me wrong—technology is a wonderful advancement. However, it is also a barrier to work–life balance, and this barrier can start at an early age. Children learn from what they are taught. Work–life balance is about time, communication, respect, and enjoying the moment, regardless of the activity.

Work–life balance has four key areas: family, career, health, and friends. May you always have equal time in each area of your life because work–life balance certainly makes you feel happy and whole.

I'm often asked whether I truly live the life that I display on social media. My answer is simple and truthful: yes. I choose not to allow others to fill my schedule, determine my decisions, or make me feel inept when I have the power to say no. Time is precious to me.

I've had an incredible life thus far. My experience with loss, trauma, and tragedy may be a bit higher on the scale of life compared to most people's experiences; however, all of it happened in my twenties and thirties and helped mold me into who I am today and give me a level of resilience that is second to none.

Losing my dad at twenty-one years of age was devastating to me as a young adult because he was my hero—a born entrepreneur who succeeded and endured through hard times. My dad parented with an "edge" and made his points clearly and concisely and always with a sharp tone. However, the intent was to be loving and help me learn lessons—many of which I learned, and sometimes the hard way.

I've learned to become a true thought leader. My work–life balance has led me to be a leader in this topic and coin myself as a work–life balance specialist, a term that most people find confusing and think of as being impossible.

Renaissance women get what I am saying, and I truly resonate with all of them I've met so far. I'm excited to meet many more, mostly because that is who I was born to be and who I am. Being articulate, intelligent, communicative, approachable, fun, honest, real, and genuine—and showing your integrity and possessing GRIT—are all traits of a work–life balance specialist.

Compare yourself to no one else. Be your original self. Be the best you can be. You are enough.

"Be yourself, everyone else is taken."—Oscar Wilde

To Contact Deb:

Phone: (519) 878-5839

Website: www.mamadeb.com

Twitter: @MamaDebCrowe

Facebook: https://www.facebook.com/MamaDebsKitchen?ref=hl

Dr. Carolyn Butler

Dr. Carolyn Butler is an Independent Leadership Coach, Speaker, and Trainer for the John Maxwell Group. As a John Maxwell Certified Coach, Teacher, and Speaker, she offers workshops, seminars, keynote speaking, and coaching, aiding personal and professional growth through practical application of John's proven leadership methods. Working together, she will move you and/or your team or organization in the desired direction to reach your goals. She has over 25 years of experience in corporate training, performance management, leadership, and organizational development. As a leadership consultant, she focuses leaders in structuring organizational vision and mission that are in alignment with the desired business outcomes. She has earned a doctorate in Organizational Leadership and a Master's Degree in Public Administration, with a specialization in Program Development & Analysis.

Dr. Butler has a real passion for guiding personal growth and self-discovery. She believes where there is no Dream there is no Hope, where there is no VISION there is no Growth. The VISION Navigator specializes in forming MasterMind groups that focus on awakening dreams and building momentum to make the dream a reality. The MasterMind forum is structured to refocus life goals and thought processes that encourage the participant to take actions that lead to success. Personal Coaching services and Seminars are available to further develop the individuals. It is through the interaction and leading of the forum that the dream of being an

The Change[5]

author was awakened within Carolyn. She has a forthcoming book entitled *Intentionally Courageous* which is her resolve to take charge of her life after a series of life-altering events.

Breakdown to Breakthrough: Live Life Intentionally Courageous

By Dr. Carolyn Butler

Breakdowns—everyone has them. They are those moments when who you are or have become is no longer effective in successfully meeting the expectations in life. Breakdowns are those points in life where you are suffering mentally, emotionally, socially, and physically. They are those points in life where beliefs, values, and assumptions are challenged. You are operating from habits, routines, and rituals which don't require much thought; just going through the motion. Then something happens that disrupts that flow. The world around you just doesn't make sense anymore.

The morning that I woke up and realized that I did not know the person looking back at me in the mirror was the scariest time in my life. A series of life events left me in a world where I was no longer a wife, a daughter, or a mother as it had been scripted for me the last 50 years. The boundaries that were invisible now were quite apparent. In the moment of breakdown, the knowledge of oneself, perception of the world, and reality all collide. You are limited, thus it seems that the suffering and discomfort is all that is left. Each traumatic event leads to dying moments—a little of who you know yourself to be dies each time. Our minds serve us just what we are ordering during these breakdowns—sorrow, pain and self-pity. In my lifetime, I have had many of these dying moments—divorce, loss of children, sexual abuse, job loss, and all my worldly possessions gone. My mother had posed a question to me some years back: Are you living or just existing? I knew the answer to the question and I answered it—I am just existing.

For several years after that moment, I was left in of place of darkness and despair. In my own secret place, I realized I had been fighting depression, loneliness, and self-doubt for years. Breakdowns can show up as thought loops that go around and around in the mind—of course leading nowhere. As I have done so many times and for so long, I placed everything in the back of my mind and moved on. I filled my life with doing stuff and staying busy so that I did not have to feel the pain. You live life just as much by what you unconsciously believe as what you consciously believe about yourself. Consciously I believe that I should have the life I dream about. After all my hard work and being a good Christian, I wasn't where I had imagined.

I have over the years read so many self-help books in order to move beyond this place, but I kept finding myself returning to where love, trust, and life ended for me. The law of attraction made sense to me and thus consciously I took action to surround myself with visuals and affirmations to get what I wanted. My perception of what the law of attraction meant was that I needed to stay focused on positive things and have an image of what I wanted to attract. My rooms began to be filled with sticky notes, posters, and vision boards. There were some positive things that happened, but not to my level of expectations. In every area of my life—finances, health, relationships, and career—it wasn't matching up to my vision board. When something positive happened in my life, I would justify the truth behind the law of attraction, even though I have accomplished not one thing on my vision board. What was my problem? After reading *The Flaw in the Law Attraction* by Jim Britt, I claimed right to sanity. The affirmations and visuals are great resources and tools, but we do have to fix what is on the inside. If I don't love myself or feel that I don't deserve to have what I want in life or if I don't understand how my words and thoughts—consciously or unconsciously…I am only going to have more of what I have been getting.

I do believe that everyone has a divine purpose. Each person has talent and skills that uniquely contribute to the fulfillment of their life's mission. When you are not living within your purpose or desire holistically, you are incomplete as an individual. You are not operating from a point of wholeness. As children, our parents raise us with their ideas, beliefs, and values. Then our thoughts are shaped and molded by work, schools, and religious organizations. Essentially, everything about us has been the thoughts and desires of someone else. Your determination to be successful comes from an internal thought process that guides you through getting the external things done. If those thoughts are not truly yours—meaning you have not affirmatively identified and developed your own set of beliefs and values—you are not being authentic. Too often, we go through life just living by the script that others have given us. It is not necessarily a bad script—it is just not yours. Success has to be defined by the individual. Unfortunately, we can get to this place where nothing has meaning to us and we care less and less about self. What you do no longer matters. We fail to really search our inner-self to determine who we are or want to be. It takes courage to dream about a better life for you. It takes living intentionally courageous to go from breakdown to breakthrough. The change has to be about you and for you.

What does an intentional courageous life look like? It is a life that is deliberately designed by you. It means approaching life responsibly and purposely, with goals mindful of who you are and about what you want out of life. It is about living consciously, being awake with intentions versus wandering and operating on biases, experiences, and expectations of others. An intentional life is one with a definite direction. It is about not accepting what we have been accepting from others as our truth without intentionally deciding that we agree. We have a specific God-given calling and purpose. We have a God-given mission. We have to be in pursuit of our mission. We must define the specific mission in our own life. Otherwise, we end up meandering aimlessly while fending off that persistent feeling of emptiness. Awakening to a new life and new meaning to life is yet another journey to begin. It feels somewhat rebellious. Everything you want to achieve in life is dependent upon you being you. That takes courage.

"The original definition of 'courage' is from the Latin word 'cor,' meaning 'heart.' And the original definition was to tell the story of who you are with your whole heart." It means being authentic to all that you were created to be. It means change. For many of us, it is going to take courage to reject dispelling, dysfunctional beliefs and paradigms about God and his purpose for us. Once you identify who you are and begin that transformation, the life you have dreamed becomes a reality. As soon as you decide to learn to live life on your terms, everything will shift and come into alignment with divine order.

It takes courage to change who you have become and where you want to be. It takes being intentionally courageous because you have to get past all the challenges that this decision will bring. For me, I had to deprogram my thoughts and get to this point in the journey and say what it is that I want out of life. Change or transformation is always about changing a mental concept. Renewing the mind is a process of dumping what is not useful and not needed in the mind. As we go through our daily life, we often add to our mind thoughts, beliefs, and ideas of others that at that moment seem quite beneficial. I venture to say that often they are beneficial for that point in our life. We can't stay stuck in that moment of time or thought. Everything around us goes through a metamorphosis—a transition or change. The universe is constantly changing direction and transforming as beliefs, culture, and people change. We witness this metamorphosis with the changing of the seasons. It happens naturally…plant life and animal life accepts these changes and with each cycle begins a new beginning…but much stronger and steadier than before. Humankind seems to have the worst time making these transitions through life. In my quest to do me, I have decided to experience life and grow. I am deciding for myself what things I enjoy doing and what things I don't. I decree and declare that I can do anything I want in this life and so can you. It is time for my breakthrough. Breakthrough simply means breaking through any obstacles or blocks that are holding you back.

Are you wandering through life aimlessly, with little passion for living or purpose? In life, you not only attract what you believe about the things you want, but more importantly what you believe about yourself. What you believe about yourself determines the value you place on life and what you want and get out of life. Whether it is through words spoken to you or around you as a child…or through life experiences—this shapes who you are.

Are you one of those people who has put your life on hold to accommodate other people, whether it is spouse, children, or friends? What happens when you find yourself alone? What happens when things that kept you occupied are no longer there? I believe everyone has a dream, but those dreams for many of us go left unfulfilled. We settle back in life and take what we believe it has to offer. I was taught if you have a roof over your head, a job, and a reasonable portion of health and strength, then I should be content. We are afraid to question people of authority; we are afraid to question our parents; we are afraid to question God or at least what we are taught about God and our life. In order to get back to some degree of normalcy, we have to stop projecting our habitual assumptions and start to see reality—start living intentionally. Are you ready for your breakthrough? That leads us to the question…What does breakthrough look like for you? Living life intentionally is when you live your life congruently with your personalities, skills, and desires, regardless of how the majority around you are living.

It is going to take courage to face the fears of the past that have shaped and molded the person we have become. When I started on the journey, I was looking for a way to become the best version of myself. At the start the journey, it looked as easy as writing affirmations daily and plotting pictures on my vision board. The inner self was not strong enough to shine through all the darkness inside and outside of me. How you are interpreting the world impacts your senses where you are generalizing, deleting, or distorting information based on your perception.

Here are five manageable steps to incorporate into your life plan to help keep your dreams and visions alive—and pave a path toward finding God's destined purpose for your life:

1. Hire a Coach. If you are truly serious about making changes in your life, you need someone who will provide you with the real thought provoking questions. Most of the things in your life right now is not enough because you will hear the same messages that you have heard that have got you where you are today. That is not to say that where you are is a bad place. You could be like me; if I did nothing else, I am happy and celebrate my accomplishments. I want more out of life. I want my life to reflect my new standards and values based on my renewed mind-set. Coaches assist you with being aware of the current situation and then deciding on an outcome that's in alignment with who you are.

2. Be intentional in your walk into this moment of clarity. It doesn't require you to reject everything that you have learned and believe. It does require you to deliberately question what you have accepted as truth. Everything needs to evolve into your truth. In the ontological coaching approach, you are focused on your present state.

3. Be Courageous. This is a new person that has a new walk and talk. People are not receptive of change and will only know the old ways and behavior. You have to be willing to move from the core of who you are and live that life, regardless of who it offends or who declares they don't like the new you. You have to be determined to tell the story.

4. Have a visual outcome and plan of Action. Every day, do something that moves you closer. Choosing to do nothing or wander is an outcome.

5. Research your vision. You are the master of your destiny, thus whatever this will require in terms of knowledge and skill, you do it diligently. A simply strategy to keep in mind is to do one positive thing each day that takes you closer to that vision. Think progress, not perfection. Use a dream journal. Follow the advice in God's word: "Write the vision, and make it plain…" (Habakkuk 2:2) Writing about your dreams and goals will keep them alive, even when nothing seems to be happening. It is the best way to stay focused on your desires and filter out anything that encroaches upon your ideas and thoughts.

There has been some definite changes in my lifestyle, some prioritizing, some behavioral changes, some belief changes, and commitment changes. See, I get to decide what is successful in my life, not anyone else. As I get closer, the picture is getting clearer. Having been where most people are today and will continue to be, I know the challenge. We Christians use the word—or I should say misuse the word—content. You spend most of your day talking about your dream or thinking about your dream and in reality that is all it is ever going to be—a dream. There is no moving forward because we convince ourselves to be content or settle for what we have if it is not bad. We should be GRATEFUL or at least understand that CONTENT doesn't mean SETTLING.

I have not come this far to allow people, time, and my ignorance to rob me of the Good Things God has in store for me. I will not do that and you shouldn't either...We are Masterpieces in progress or I am moving FORWARD.

Along the way, things get in the way of our movement forward; there are disappointments, discouragement, and the outcome of reality. Sometimes that reality is that we are LOST. One moment the adrenaline is pumping through the veins and we are in a childlike state believing that nothing can stop us from reaching our dreams. We keep going and going and going, never checking our compass or ignoring the compass. At some point, we realize that we have not arrived at the destination, and then we stop believing that it can happen. What looked so easy when we started is no longer bringing the same type of joy. The dream is still inside and it may mean getting to a quiet place to determine where you are. The Psalmist writes "you chart the path ahead of me and tell me where to stop and rest. Every moment you know where I am" (Psalms 139:3).

God has created in us an internal compass, so we are equipped with a means to know when we are getting off course. It is comforting to know we have a Vision Navigator that knows where we are every moment and it is to him that we take time to ask for directions. In your Vision quest, move forward past the disappointments and discouragement by taking time to always reflect and determine where you are and ask for direction. No matter where you are right now...Stop and Get Direction but Stay encouraged and keep moving toward your VISION. Being aware of your present circumstances is the first step of deciding what happens next. Next step ask—seek out the help you need to continue on the journey. You might need your own Vision Navigator—someone who is not there to tell you what you want to hear or what to do.

Nobody knows what you are truly capable of doing except you. There will be plenty of times when you won't feel up to it. Even when things are good, many people don't realize their own capacity for success and it can be even more difficult to believe in our dreams when things are tough. It's important to continue to dream—because your dreams are powerful! I'm not talking about the ones in your sleep, but the musings and daydreams you consciously think about—your dreams of the future. Give yourself permission to think and live differently. Just because people in your life have their thoughts on what life is does not have to be your reality. The Truth does set you free from the patterns, habits, and rituals that are meaningless and hold you back.

Despite how bleak it looks, stay the course, keep moving and you will eventually reach your destination. You are on the edge of a breakthrough. Keep the Dream Alive. Be intentionally courageous in the pursuit of living the life you were created to have and all the things that you define as success.

To Contact Carolyn:

Website: Carolyn@thevisionnavigator.com

Vision Navigator Website: www.thevisionnavigator.com

Facebook: www.facebook.com/carolynvision.navigator

JMT website: www.johncmaxwellgroup.com/carolynbutler

Facebook: www.facebook.com/intentionallycourageous

Jeanie Cisco-Meth

Have you or a loved one felt the pain of being bullied? Have you ever wondered why people bully?

Hi,

I'm Jeanie Cisco-Meth and I wrote the book *Bully Proofing You: Improving Confidence and Personal Value from the Inside Out*.

I was a high school teacher for over 15 years and I saw the devastation that can be caused by bullies. The question is, "Why do 3 out of 4 blow it off and 1 in 4 have serious lasting affects?" I spent years answering this question and doing research so I could help myself and others deal with this trauma.

Bullying is a global problem, but the solution is individual. My program, *Bully Proofing You: Improving Confidence and Personal Value from the Inside Out* is the powerful solution to this insidious problem.

Our world can no longer pay the invoice written by bullies with the lives of our loved ones. The price tag is just too high.

I want to thank you for the opportunity to introduce *Bully Proofing You*. It has changed hundreds of lives and will continue to do so. You will see the effects of *Bully Proofing You* ripple out from your life and into your community.

Metamorphosis

By Jeanie Cisco-Meth

As I stepped off the curb into the bright sunshine, a smile spread across my face. After all, I was heading to see the man of my dreams. The day was perfect. I should know. I had been planning it since I was a young girl in high school. Now I was living it. How did I become so blessed? When did everything change for me? It wasn't always like this. I thought back to my first marriage—the pain, the fear, the insecurities, the name calling, and the infidelity had made my life miserable. I had been broken, and I didn't even know it. The problem was I didn't realize how bad it had gotten until I was free of it. The best thing he ever did for me was to give me my daughter, Erin, and ask me for a divorce. At that moment, I was free to start living my life. It was no cakewalk, believe me. I had to change everything I had become.

I had been a strong, independent woman. Now I was broken and scared to try living on my own while raising a toddler. Erin was two, and I was twenty-four. We rented a little apartment in a rundown part of town because that was all I could afford. I enrolled at the University of Utah so I could finish my degree. I had sixty-five credit hours to complete to earn my Bachelor of Science degree. I knew I had to do it while Erin was little and wouldn't remember the hard times. I knew if I didn't go to school, it would always be hard for us.

I wanted to give her everything. I didn't want her going hungry. I didn't want to be kicked out because the rent was raised, and I couldn't afford to pay it. I wanted to be able to send Erin to her prom wearing a new dress. I knew the only way to make sure those things happened was to get an education and a career.

I finished sixty-five credit hours in three terms. A full-time load is considered twelve credit hours a term. I got three to four hours of sleep a night and sometimes not even that much. On the weekends, I worked nights and would try to get some sleep while Erin sat on my chest and watched cartoons.

There were times I wanted to quit—times I wanted to give up. Then there were times I knew we would make it. I learned how to focus on now. Focus on what I had to do right now to get to the next right now. If I looked into the future, I would get scared and overwhelmed. I would lose my way, and my steps would falter. It helped me to keep moving forward to the next moment, because in the next moment, I was creating the life I wanted.

Some days, I felt like I was crawling on my hands and knees just to keep going. My perspective was that I knew I could do whatever it took to get what I wanted. I just needed to keep moving forward one step at a time.

I spent some time thinking about how I had gotten to where I was. I realized I had created the mess, so it was up to me to create a good life.

I know my thoughts and beliefs create my reality. I also know I can't control anyone else, and no matter how much I want things to change, I must change them myself.

That spring, as graduation day came closer and closer, I knew I was going to make it. I went to every event offered to graduating seniors. The lunch at the university president's manor, the field trip, the class ring—I enjoyed all of it. When I walked across the stage to receive my diploma, I did the happy dance. Everyone said they wanted to do something crazy or special, but when it came time to make the trip in front of the crowd, they chickened out. Not me! If I could have done cartwheels, I would have. I had worked so hard for this day, and it meant so much to me. My daughter and family were in the crowd watching, and I didn't want to contain myself. I just felt I had to let what I was feeling on the inside show on the outside.

I learned that if you're a little crazy and push your comfort zone, you inspire others to do the same. I had people I had never met before come up to me and say they had wanted to do something fun, but just didn't have the nerve. I asked them if next time they would be more likely to let their feelings show. They all said yes, but I'm not sure they ever did. You see, stepping outside your comfort zone takes practice. Start small. Take a small step every day so that the next time you want to do something fun, you have the courage to do it. Every time you shrink back, you build that wall higher and thicker. Every time you push through, you weaken the wall around your comfort zone, and it becomes easier for you to keep moving forward.

If you want something you don't have, you need to grow. You need to get outside your comfort zone and find it. The only things in your comfort zone are the things you currently have. That's why it's called your comfort zone. It holds everything you're comfortable with.

My ex-husband had forced me out of my comfort zone a year before, and now my life was better because of it. I don't think I ever would have left him because of where I was in my mind at the time. But when he said, "We need to end this," I was all for it. Something inside me clicked and said, "Yes, that's what I want as well. I don't want to live this way anymore. It's time for a change." I learned to stop trying to fix him and just work on myself. I learned you can't change anyone but yourself.

I can help people who ask for it, and I can show them the way, but they must take action to make the changes they want.

Not too long after graduation, I was working three jobs, and things were not going as I had planned. I hadn't gotten a teaching job, so I was still waiting tables at Dee's restaurant, working the night shift. That is where I met my second husband. He lived in a wonderful house with his mother, who was dying of cancer. He helped take care of her. His father had died earlier that year, and he needed someone to love him and care for him. He needed a mother. I didn't realize that until after we were married. He gave me my incredible son, Max.

I learned that people are not always honest. They might mean well, but actions speak louder than words. I learned that the "why" for changing has to be bigger than anything else, because change is hard. When the pain of change is beating on you every day, remember your "why" for wanting to make the change—and the blows aren't as tough to withstand.

I had started a teaching career and loved it. It helped me withstand the problems in my marriage. I wanted to help others the way I had received help in school. I had so many learning disabilities that I was told I would never amount to much because I would never make it through school. There were teachers that helped me make it and I desired to do the same for my students.

About two years into my second marriage, we had a family picture taken. I looked at that picture and was shocked at what I saw in my eyes and face. The change had been so gradual I hadn't noticed it until it was literally staring me in the face.

My mother asked me, "If Erin was in this type of relationship, would you want her to stay?"

"No," I said. The answer was clear. It was time to make a change.

I spent some time soul searching to figure out what I had done wrong, because the only common element of the two marriages was me. I learned I had settled in both of my marriages. I knew what I wanted, but I had gotten tired of waiting for it to come along. I thought what I had was good enough. I thought I could make things work. I thought I was being unreasonable. "I'll never find what I'm looking for so I might as well just get used to it being like this," I told myself.

I learned to never settle.

I asked myself what I wanted from life and my marriage. I took time to plan it all out—the man and how he would treat my kids and me. The way we would talk about the difficult things. The fun we would have together. The way it would feel when he kissed me. I could see the look in his eyes when I walked into a room. I felt the tenderness he would show my children while correcting them. He had to enjoy cooking because I didn't like it. His strengths would complement my weaknesses. Together, we would be a powerful team plowing our way through life and its adventures. I knew everything about him. I just didn't know how he would look or where I'd meet him.

I decided to give Match.com a try. I lived out in Eagle Mountain City Center, Utah with not too many eligible bachelors around. My first ex-husband was my safety net. He was much better as a friend than he had ever been as a husband. I would let him know I was going to meet someone, what his name was, where, and what time we were meeting. He would give me a call about fifteen minutes into the meeting to make sure I was safe. It also gave me an out if I needed to leave. The lesson that not everyone is honest kept coming up, and I knew I could leave with an excuse and not have to confront him about it. Let someone else deal with that problem. I had already learned that life is too short to waste it wishing someone were different. I had made the decision that if the person wasn't perfect for me, I would move on. I knew exactly what I was looking for.

You could say I had a shopping list, and if he didn't have the qualities on my list, he could look elsewhere. I had traveled that road already, and I was not going down it again.

Erin's dad came by to pick her up one weekend, and he wanted to learn more about Match.com. I told him what it was and how it worked. I showed him my profile and the matches it had for me. He asked me about the gentlemen at the top of the list, the one I had been skipping over many times because he didn't look the way I thought he should. He had a goatee a lot like Max's dad, and I just didn't want to go there. Erin's dad said, "You should contact him. He looks honest." So I did.

I sent Laurence a message inviting him to look over my profile and get in touch with me if he wanted to. We corresponded through e-mail and instant messenger for about a month. Then we exchanged phone numbers. The first time I heard his voice, he had gone to Colorado to visit his friends for a Halloween party. I was nervous and excited. He told me later that when he hung up the phone, he thought I was either a lot of fun or on drugs. He really wasn't sure what to think. We spent the next three months talking on the phone and laying a foundation for what was to come.

I didn't see his face in person until after my birthday in January. That was almost four months after we had first made contact. I remember walking into the Denny's in American Fork thinking, "If nothing else, we are going to be great friends." I was in a hurry because I was meeting him during a short break from school. We only had thirty minutes for lunch in those days, and we were to stay with our students. I asked a fellow teacher to cover my classroom until I got back. She was as excited for me as I was. She wanted to see how it would turn at as well. I had been telling her about Match.com from the beginning. Now was the moment of truth. What would be next for Laurence and me?

The Change[5]

I have laser-like focus when I have a target, and Laurence was my target that day. I walked into Denny's and saw him sitting at a table. I walked up, sat down, and started telling him how I only had a few minutes because I had to get back to the classroom. When I stopped to take a breath, he said, "Well, I'm Laurence." The look on my face must have been priceless because I said, "Of course you are." Then it struck me. What if I had sat down at the wrong table? I had only seen his profile picture, and those aren't very good quality. It could have happened. I'm so glad I sat down at the right table!

We were married on October 13, 2002, just 366 days after we had met online. He is everything I wanted and more. He is perfect for me and for my family. We have had our struggles and bumps, raising four children together and dealing with four exes. Both of us have been married twice before with a child from each marriage.

Believe me, I'm not perfect, and he's not perfect, but together we are close to perfect. He is exactly what I dreamed up when I took the time to figure out what I really wanted—and found the patience to wait for it. Now, twelve years later, my relationship is incredible. I learned I create my life with my thoughts, feelings, decisions, and actions. I love my life. I'm not sure how perfect gets better, but it does. There are days I think I couldn't love him any more than I do right now and then it happens. I do. We keep growing and learning and our relationship keeps evolving to better understanding and an even deeper love. I'm excited for the next sixty-four years. Of course I'll be 112 by then, but that's OK. We promised each other we would beat my great-grandparents' record of seventy-five years. I think we can do it. If anyone can, we can.

I have learned life is what you make it. Wherever you are right now, you created that. If you want to create something new, you have to do that as well. It all starts with believing you're worth it. Believe you deserve what you want. Listen to the voices that lift you up and encourage you. Shut off the voices that bring you down and make you feel bad. Both of them are your voice. Both of them are in your head. You control them. You decide which one to listen to, and if you listen to the negative one, that's what you'll get—a negative life.

I hope you don't have to go through two divorces to learn what I did. You are free to learn from my mistakes. In fact, I suggest you do. It's less painful that way. Take a moment and evaluate where you are and where you want to be. If they aren't the same thing, you need to make some changes. You can do this. I know you can. Believe me, if I can do it, you can do it. All it takes is a high personal value, a new perspective, some planned responses, and practice. If you have and do all of these things, you too will be stepping off the curb into your dream life.

If you need help, look around you. There are people just waiting for you to ask for help. But remember what they tell you is just advice. You choose whether to follow it or not. If they have walked the path before you, they might have some valuable information for you. If they haven't, beware. You are the one that will live with the consequences of your decisions, not them. Listen to what they have to say, but make your own decision about what to do. One thing you need to remember about advice is that everyone loves to give it, but not everyone can take it. Also remember that you decide how your story goes. Others will influence you, but nothing is their fault. It is all on you. Make a decision today about what you want. Now take the first small step toward creating it. Hummingbird-size steps count, too. You might have to low-crawl a time or two, but you'll get there. Keep moving forward and don't settle. The highway of life is dotted with many parking spaces. Make sure you're in the one you want. If not, back out, and get moving again. Take your loved ones along if you can. If you can't, you'll find new loved ones along the way. Just make sure they are the ones you want and need.

If you don't make the changes you need to make, you'll find yourself in the same position you were in before. I have learned that no matter where I go, there I am. If I want to go someplace new, I have to become someone new. Stretch your comfort zone so you can grow into the person you were meant to be.

Look me up and let me know how it's going. I'd love to hear your story. You've heard mine, so it's only fair. Take the first step right now to creating your dream life, and in a few years you'll be glad you did. You have to start to finish, so get started making your change now.

To Contact Jeanie:

www.jeanieciscometh.com

www.bullyproofingyou.com

jeanie@jeanieciscometh.com

Facebook: jeanieciscometh or bullyproofingyou

Podcast: Bully Proofing U on iTunes

Twitter: @jeaniemeth

Google+: Jeanieciscometh

Julie Anne Jones

Julie Anne Jones is a sought-after keynote speaker, ICF Accredited life and business coach, trainer, and the CEO of Julie Anne Jones, Inc. Known as "the systems queen," she can break down just about any concept or big picture problem into doable steps. She teaches simple systems that work for anyone. Training topics include personal development, coaching and mentoring skills, leadership, women's empowerment, and social media business-building tools.

Over the past eight years, she's been blessed to have had the privilege of bringing her training to corporate events throughout the United States and Canada. Julie Anne is most at home when she's on stage and she loves sharing her information, whether it's from a live stage, through her popular Direct Sales Virtual Academy, her webinar and tele-seminar training platforms, or her weekly blog posts. She not only tells her audiences what to do and how it will improve their results, she also breaks things down and gives her audience simple tools and language to implement those concepts.

Since 2009, Julie Anne has been creating online programs and products and has used the power of social engagement to build a multiple six-figure income from her computer.

Solving the Myth of "Overwhelm" Using the Triple D Approach

By Julie Anne Jones

Your home office is a disaster. You're overwhelmed! Your calendar is jammed with too much to do. You're overwhelmed! Your house is a mess, dinner's burning, and your kid just informed you that he needs three dozen cupcakes for a class party tomorrow (when did they start celebrating National Kid's Day anyhow?). Now you're SUPER overwhelmed! Have you noticed how just saying that out loud somehow makes it seem okay that nothing's getting done or (worse) that nothing is changing in your life or business?

Over the past ten years in my work as a business coach and trainer, I've heard those two words more times than I can count. Especially for women (who tend to take on too much in every area of their lives), it's easy to default to the helpless (and hopeless) space that's encompassed in being overwhelmed. It's almost as if, by claiming your place in the "overwhelmed" line, you have an excuse for the chaos in your life and lack of results in your business.

It really bothered me when I first started coaching. As a coach, my job is to support my clients in figuring out exactly what they want, then taking action to get it. Time and again, I'd see clients going nowhere, stuck in "overwhelm." I began to realize that it's actually a myth to say you're overwhelmed, and I developed a simple system to walk my clients through that mythical land of "overwhelm" to the results that they wanted.

The truth is, "overwhelmed" is nothing more than a state of mind that you can choose in any given moment. It's not the circumstances in your environment or your life that make you overwhelmed, but the choice you make to BE overwhelmed that causes you grief. By throwing up your hands in that moment of declaration and choosing the overwhelmed mind-set, you're actually substituting results for a really good excuse. You're also robbing yourself of the motivation to change your circumstances or the way you're looking at them.

It's paralyzing in the worst way.

When one of my clients tells me they're overwhelmed, I immediately ask them what's making them feel that way. Surprisingly, they often can't answer that question without further prodding and poking from me. They're so stuck that they can't even see what's holding them back. They've so completely committed to "being overwhelmed" that they've lost sight of what's causing them to feel that way. It sounds incredible but it's absolutely true. That's because overwhelm by its very nature gives you an excuse not to take action. It encourages you to simply spin and complain in the powerlessness of the overwhelm definition without doing anything to change your circumstances. It might be painful, but it's easier than actually DOING SOMETHING!

When you don't take action, you don't get results. Results are what everybody I've ever met *claims* they want. Setting goals and making plans for the results you want is easy. Taking action and proactively moving toward that result is much more difficult. That requires self-discipline and motivation. You have to hold yourself accountable for the outcome you've claimed you want.

Too often, when the going gets a little tough, people are willing to settle for a good excuse instead of pushing forward to get what they want. But here's the thing. A good excuse plus no results never equals results. You may feel better in the moment by using the "I'm overwhelmed" excuse, but in the long run, it robs you of the joy of actually attaining what you want.

The Change[5]

Now that we've clearly identified the absolute myth of "I'm Overwhelmed," what can we do to change that choice? Well, if admitting you have a problem is the first step, then conceding that you're not actually overwhelmed, but instead you're just choosing to identify your current circumstances in that way is where you start. Just be willing to consider that you may not be overwhelmed. Redefine your state of mind to "very busy" or "completely involved" in this moment.

For me, just saying that to myself often totally changes the way I feel about my current circumstances. I'll often say something like, "I'm cooking with HIGH HEAT today!" It energizes me to get through that to-do list, even if the things on the list aren't necessarily things I'm thrilled about doing. So first, make a choice to identify your state of mind in a more positive way.

Then, specifically look for what it is you *think* is making you feel overwhelmed. Sit down and write out a list of everything you have to do (since too much to do is usually what we mean when we say we are overwhelmed). Don't hold back. Let yourself brain dump anything you can think of, from emptying the garbage to finishing your novel. Nothing is too big or too small.

At the end of this process, you'll have a real, true read on what you actually have on your plate. What I've found as a coach (with literally zero exceptions), is that once you're confronted with that list, it puts things into measurable perspective and you realize you were blowing those "to dos" completely out of proportion. Either that or you have ridiculously unrealistic expectations for yourself regarding what you need to do within a certain time frame. Either way, a solution begins to appear that will get you moving. You can now make a plan and start acting on it.

Let me give you an example. I had a coaching call recently with a client who was planning a trip overseas. She came to the call (in her words) "completely overwhelmed" and couldn't possibly see how she'd get it all done. We started to make her list...pack, go to the bank, change her voicemail, stop her mail, hire a pet sitter, etc. Admittedly, it was a pretty long list. But once we started to break down how long each item on that list would actually take her to complete, she started to see a light at the end of the tunnel.

In her panicked state of mind and without actually defining what she needed to do, she was letting herself believe that each item on her list (the one that was only living in her head prior to this exercise) was going to take forever to complete. When I asked her "What can you do today?" she said "Pack." "How long will that take you?" I asked. She thought about it for a minute and said, "An hour, two tops." I reminded her that it was only 9:00 in the morning, so she could be done packing before lunch and move on to the next item on her list.

Once she put "packing" in proper perspective, it shrank by several hours. It helped her to see that it really wasn't as big a deal as she'd blown it up to be in her "overwhelmed" state of mind. As we worked through the rest of the items on her list, she began to realize something very interesting. Not only could she get everything done in plenty of time to be ready to leave on her trip (which was over a week away), but she could do it while still taking care of the day-to-day activities in her life that needed her attention. And, more importantly, she could do it without feeling overwhelmed and powerless.

Realistically look at everything on the to-do list you've made and create a clear plan for how long each item will take you to accomplish. Then get a ballpark idea of when you'll do it. Once you shine the light on your list and look at it through objective, realistic eyes, your whole perspective can (and usually will) shift. With that plan in place, you can begin taking action from a place of calm and control instead of the chaotic, chicken-with-your-head-cut-off energy that's brought on by declaring that you're overwhelmed.

But what if your list truly *is* too long to realistically get everything done that you need to get done in the amount of time you have to do it? Then it's okay to officially declare yourself as "overwhelmed," right? Only if you want to stay stuck with no results (and who wants that, really?) So first, make sure you really do have too much to do and that this isn't just your round-about way of dodging the action items on your list.

If you determine that it really is the case, you'll want to employ what I call the "Triple D" formula. I've used this formula with my clients for years and it's a fast and easy way to solve your overwhelm dilemma. It's a simple, three-step formula where you'll quickly determine what items on your list you can Delete, Delegate, or Defer to narrow it down so that it's more doable and less "overwhelming."

Delete

Let's start with the "delete button." Chances are good, if you've truly brain dumped and written down everything that you *think* you need to get done, there are some items on your list that you could let go of. I find that often, when I feel like I've got too much to do, it's because I'm crowding my plate with things I don't really *need* to do. Maybe catching the news tonight or calling my friend isn't important this week. Get out a marker and go through your list, looking for what you can remove from it. Be brutal. Taking it off your list now doesn't mean you can never do it again. It's just an activity you're deleting for now in the interest of time.

Delegate

The second "D" stands for "delegate." If you're a super achiever (and chances are good, if you're reading this book, that you fall into that category), delegating is easier said than done. I speak from experience. I used to think it was easier for me to "just do it myself" than it was to take the time to ask someone to do it for me. Plus, if I'm honest, I generally think I'll do a better job if I do it myself.

As a woman, asking for help isn't one of my strong suits, even with people I've actually hired to help me. Let's face it, in order to delegate, you have to be willing to let go of control and trust someone else to pick up the slack and take on the task. That's a challenge for most of us. Understanding that is the first step toward doing it anyway.

Learning to delegate is one of the greatest skills I have ever cultivated and it has been truly life changing for me. Plus, I learned something important as I got better and better at asking for help. When you ask someone for help, it's a huge compliment to them. This is especially true if you're someone who rarely asks for help or seems to have it "all together" to an outsider looking in. More than once, I've had the person I'm asking for help tell me they were honored that I'd asked them. It's a pretty awesome side effect to learning to delegate and a whole new perspective for those of us doing the asking.

Let's go back to that list you made earlier. Ask yourself specifically what you could delegate and to whom you could delegate it. Could you have your husband pick up the dry cleaning or ask your assistant to take over your email? You'll be amazed at the things you can quickly cross off of your list when you start to ask others to take them on. Will they be done as perfectly as you might have done them? Probably not. But they'll be done. Most of the time, that's much more important. So empower the people in your life by asking them for help.

Defer

Finally, are there things on your list that you can defer until later? Can you put off getting your haircut or painting your bedroom until sometime down the road when you don't have so much to do? Probably. If you truly have a lot to do, putting off the less important things is a smart tactic for moving out of overwhelm almost immediately. Those things on your list that feel urgent really aren't important and can steal valuable time from what really needs to get done.

Unfortunately, I often find that things that end up on my defer list are things that I don't really mind doing. It's easy to distract myself from the more important, bigger, often more involved or difficult things on my list by focusing on the menial things that are basically "no brainers." If you're busy, you have to make sure you're spending your time on high-value activities. The rest can wait. You'll be surprised at what you can eliminate and how quickly your list gets narrowed down as you work through this step.

So let's review. First, hopefully you understand now what you're *actually* doing when you declare that you're "overwhelmed." More importantly, you see how destructive it is and how it absolutely doesn't serve you. You understand that a good excuse ("I'm overwhelmed!") is no substitute for actual results. You can see now that "overwhelmed" is nothing more than a state of mind and that you can make a choice to be something other than overwhelmed the next time you start to move in that direction.

Hopefully you'll get out a pen and paper and brain dump that huge to-do list in your head the next time you start to feel overwhelmed. Once it's out on paper, it will probably look a lot smaller and less overwhelming. Then you can proactively begin to make some choices about how you'll handle the items on the list. You can decide on a plan based on how much time each item will take you and move forward from that new mind-set.

And finally, if you find that your list really is a little too overwhelming, you can make some deliberate choices using the "Triple D" formula. You can delete, delegate, and defer some of the items on your list, ending up with one that's doable and feels much less overwhelming. I'm not saying you'll never feel overwhelmed again, but hopefully the next time you find yourself about to mutter those two words "I'm overwhelmed!" you'll stop and think about what you're *really* saying and what you might actually do about it.

The results you'll create in that moment you make a different choice could completely change your life.

To contact Julie:

Website: http://julieannejones.com

Facebook: http://facebook.com/julieannejonesinc

Twitter: http://twitter.com/julieannejones

LinkedIn: http://linkedin.com/in/julieannejones

Email: jaj@julieannejones.com

Telephone: 509-526-3837

Rich Perry

Rich graduated from King's College with a degree in Psychology. He worked as a therapist for seven years in children's mental and behavioral health, initially concentrating on pre-teen behavioral clients and later transitioning to early development within the Autism spectrum. Rich served four years as program director for a therapeutic summer camp. Needing a change for himself, he began studying with The Tad James Co., and received certifications in Neuro-Linguistic Programming, Time Line Therapy®, and Hypnotherapy. He started his own coaching business focusing on personal and professional development, training, and motivational speaking. In addition to coaching, Rich is a musician and co-owner of Sector One Entertainment, a company whose goal is to bring music, art, and culture to the forefront of the community. Through community projects and events, his company has donated more than $15,000 to local and national charities. Rich writes a weekly mind and body column for NEPAscene.com. He's an Eagle Scout, a Vigil Honor Member, and serves as an adult leader for his home Boy Scout troop. He is a Freemason, and believes in serving others within his community. His personal motto is simple: lead by example through excellence.

Transform Pebbles into Mountains

By Rich Perry

What is this alluring thing we call success and how does one achieve it? Is it granted to a few special people, or can anyone attain it? Does it come after years of hard work and sacrifice, or is there an easier way? How can some people seemingly create the life that dreams are made of out of nowhere; does the universe favor these individuals, or are they privy to an exclusive cosmic secret?

In this chapter, I'll offer inspirational words on how to accomplish such amazing feats, to attain personal triumphs, rise to astonishing heights, and stand atop the proverbial mountain. Yet, can every day be filled with award ceremonies or million dollar deals? Is it possible to reach perfection in such a way so that you've won before your feet even touch the floor in the morning? I don't know. But what I do know is something that I learned a long time ago; so if you're all ready and willing, I'd invite you to join me on a hero's path of how to transition from momentary victories into monumental triumphs by learning to transform pebbles into mountains.

Consider this quote by Sir Winston Churchill, words that have resonated with me for many years: "Success is the ability to go from one failure to another with no loss of enthusiasm." I love this quote and it's kept me motivated through many endeavors. While I wouldn't be so brash as to change these immortal words of inspiration, I have added my own touch for personal use: "*There is no failure, only feedback* (a presupposition of Neuro-Linguistic Programming)." Together, these words have reminded me to utilize life's happenings as a learning opportunity, and encouraged me to move gracefully and enthusiastically between every situation presented. By transforming my perspective, I stopped viewing things as "pass versus fail" and started to see each new experience as an opportunity for discovery, a way to gain a valuable resource or skill and, in many cases, a moment of victory. I decided to have fun with my learnings, and as I acquired each one, I used my mind to transform it into a pebble—and I started collecting!

Before we focus on mental transmutation, it's important to note what, many times, comes beforehand and is crucial for igniting the fire that drives us towards our goal. Coincidentally—or not—I feel this spark comes in the form of recognizing the need and desire for change within our *self* that is ultimately necessary in order to begin the overall process of change.

I realized this need for change within myself two years ago. I was working as a therapist in children's mental and behavioral health and my job was to utilize therapeutic interventions in both the home and school settings, to help transfer skills to parents and school staff. The job was extremely rewarding initially, but as the years went by, the politics of the healthcare system began to weigh heavily and I was no longer satisfied with my position. More than that, I wasn't satisfied with myself because I felt like I wasn't making good use of my talents and living up to my full potential.

It was during this time that I hit an extremely low point. I was no longer the happy-go-lucky person that I used to be. I had doubts. My self-talk was regularly negative and demeaning. In my eyes, I was a hollow shell of the person I knew myself to be and I didn't even recognize my *self* in the mirror. Most of all, I was becoming depressed and I feared that my only recourse was medication, something that I resorted to in my senior year of college and I swore to never allow again. I was at a loss and didn't know what to do— and then I remembered a conversation I had with a dear friend months prior.

The Change[5]

My old college roommate Laura told me about a training program she had gone through and stated it was a life-changing experience. The training had given her a clear sense of self, life fulfillment, purpose, and she had recently left her job to start her own business as a life coach. During our friendly catch-up, I told her I was considering a change, but didn't know what I wanted or needed to do, and she encouraged me to consider becoming a coach as well. She supported this by affirming that my degree in psychology, knack for relating to people, and entrepreneurial spirit would allow for a smooth transition into coaching. Since the day we met, Laura and I had grown to be like sister and brother and I knew that she only wanted what was best for me, but even that wasn't initially enough to guide me out of my self-imposed darkness. I buried the advice under fake smiles and a continued façade of having my *shtuff* together.

One gloomy winter day, I finally had enough. I broke down at work, asked for a few minutes to compose myself, and called my friend Laura to ask for help. I asked her to tell me about her experience with the training she had mentioned months earlier. After listening to her describe this dreamlike and transformational program, I knew this could be the change I needed. There was just one problem: this training was on the opposite side of the country and I didn't have the money to pay for it; I didn't even have the money to fly out there.

By the end of our discussion, she had assured me that the money necessary to fund this particular crossing towards change was just a minor detail, and the important thing was to stay focused on the goal. To better reinforce the goal, she guided me through a process that I later came to know as Time Line Therapy® and The Secret of Creating Your Future® as created by Dr. Tad James. A technique of trance work, I followed her words precisely as she guided me towards fully experiencing the desired goal, internally of course, but my mind made it real and come to life. I couldn't believe what had just happened; within a few minutes, everything clicked! All things quickly became aligned, the future was brighter with magnificent clarity, and I was driven to reach my goal. And, most importantly, I had my first pebble.

Closely tied to recognizing this need and desire for change, it's undeniably essential to dive deep into the self, through meditation or simply being completely and entirely honest with your true self, determining if this change is something you genuinely and unconditionally want. I say it in this way because the majority of people want to change, but so few follow through. Look at any local gym at the start of the New Year. Memberships skyrocket as thousands in your city exclaim, *"This year is going to be different!"* and they dedicate themselves daily, for at least the first few weeks, to getting in shape. By March, many of those gyms that were action-packed weeks earlier are back to the normal population.

Please understand that those who fell off the treadmill (pun intended) had admirable intentions and they *did* want to change, but they simply *wanted* to want change. They wanted change because it was convenient and they received a good deal on a gym membership. They wanted change because it was time to make a New Year's Resolution and that's the thing to do. They wanted change because they hoped they could do better than last year's goal that they never accomplished. The New Year always brings that cry for change, and flooding the masses with verve to go out and finally do the things they didn't do last year, but as Albert Einstein so eloquently stated, "The definition of insanity is doing the same thing over and over again and expecting different results." While the goals may change, the underlying process and behavior remain the same, and sure enough once the hoopla fades those who only wanted to want change are left to uncover their own source of energy and motivation; just as they needed a reason to make a resolution, they are quick to find reasons to excuse themselves from continuing the task.

If you haven't done so already, take a moment and ask yourself, *"What is it that I truly want and what am I willing to do to get it?"* Are you willing to give one hundred percent of yourself to the process, one hundred percent of the time, in order to see it to the end and achieve your goal? Allow those last words to resonate with you: You must be willing to give all of yourself, all of the time. If you give one hundred percent of yourself but you're only willing to give it fifty percent of the time, or you're only willing to play the game *most of the time*, that's not enough to win. Putting on a uniform and playing most of the game doesn't make championship teams; similarly, giving a partial effort in life won't allow you to surpass your wildest dreams.

Once you are willing to completely give yourself to the process and have full belief in yourself and your ability to create the exact future you want, you too will notice that shift as all the events leading up to the successful completion of your goal begin to realign themselves. For me, within a few hours of speaking with my dear friend Laura, the answer to *"How am I going to fund this training?"* came to light and I was well on my way towards creating the life I wanted. And, I had my second pebble.

The time will come when you recognize that burning desire within yourself, as it illuminates the air around you, bathes you in warmth, orchestrates all sounds to your personal melody, and guides you on your path towards fulfilling your destiny. Maybe this has already happened and you simply needed some extra inspiration or motivation before beginning your personal expedition of excellence—in which case, take your moment and own it. Make it alive, make it real and, most of all, make it yours.

As you prepare for the journey ahead, I encourage you to be mindful of your self-talk. What is it that you tell yourself as you work towards completing specific tasks? Do you practice positive, meaningful, and motivating self-talk or are your words counterproductive, or even destructive? Much of this negative self-talk comes in the form of limiting decisions and limiting beliefs. Simply put, these are the decisions and beliefs held that impede our abilities and true potential. They can be either internally constructed or accepted and adopted from outside sources; nevertheless, they don't serve you or your purpose.

One of the first tasks I encourage clients to do as we begin the coaching process is to become mindful of self-talk, to keep a journal of thoughts both positive and serving, along with those which are negative and not serving to the individual. Do you frequently find yourself thinking or saying, *"I can do this"* or *"Yes, I deserve this opportunity"* or does your self-talk prevent you from fulfilling your desires with such statements as, *"I wish I could do this, but it's just too hard for me"* or *"I wish I was good enough to have this opportunity, but I'll never be that successful"*?

Limiting beliefs and limiting decisions can be a tricky lot and are sometimes accepted or adopted as they sneak past us under the disguise of advice from others, even those closest to us. I do not suggest that these words are malicious or that the speaker is to be perceived as an arch villain plotting your demise; in fact, many of these people have good intentions. However, it's important to be mindful of these outside suggestions and determine whether the messages are beneficial and serving or whether they should be rejected and deleted. If it's the latter, give yourself permission to do so. I repeat: give yourself permission to reject and delete the messages that do not serve your higher purpose. If you've allowed the limitations of others to influence your ability to perform in the past, STOP! Choose to trust yourself and your ability, starting now.

For example, if you're a "Grade-A Student" preparing for an exam and a "C+ Student" tells you that s/he took the test and it was the hardest test of the year, would you accept and believe it to be true, or would you choose to dismiss his or her words and enter the classroom relaxed and ready because you know that you've been studying and you are fully confident in your ability to get high marks?

Your mind is a double-edged sword and you can allow its power to serve and motivate you or you can let your imagination get the best of you, leaving you impotent to act. In America, we have a popular expression, *"to make a mountain out of a molehill,"* which essentially means to be faced with a trivial matter or minor obstacle, but to perceive it as a major disaster; in light of the theme in this chapter we might say it is the act of *"making boulders out of stones."* If examined too closely, that stone could appear to be a huge boulder, but if you take a step back and give yourself a moment to breathe, the proper perspective could help reveal the true nature of the problem and offer the appropriate solution.

I've had a fascination with the story of the underdog since childhood, the person who is able to overcome the odds despite a series of battles as he or she realizes his or her full potential and transforms into the hero we know that person to be, finally claiming a rightful place as champion. Every culture, from ancient to pop, has its own fantastic stories of conquest, but what happens when the embers have emitted their final glow, the book has closed, or the movie credits rolled? Are these stories only told to children to tuck them in at night, or are they much more than that? Can we, as adults, use them as divine inspiration as we set out on our own hero's journey? What separates the people who take initiative and seize every opportunity from those who decide to wait for the next chance because *"it's not the right time"* or they're *"too busy"* or any other *"reasonable"* excuse they allow themselves to believe?

The majority of these stories have the same basic formula. Many times, the heroes-aren't born into the role of distinction; at a certain point of passage, they transform and assume the responsibility. Over the course of their journey, they have collected resources and skills that allowed them a few small victories, but somewhere along the way something happened and the underdogs began to believe in their own ability, which marks the birth and transformation into the hero. In this respect, you should begin to reflect on past victories, no matter how small, and begin to accumulate accolades of varying types. Like our champion of modest origins, as you pile these seemingly small successes higher and higher, the once individual moments will begin to bond and reinforce each other's strength, creating a mountain of greatness.

The power of belief in one's self is incredibly profound and influential on what we do and do not achieve. Henry Ford said, "Whether you think you can, or you think you can't, you're right." If you don't recognize and believe in your own ability, it doesn't matter how many trainings you attend, which books you read, or how many affirmations you tell yourself because you're choosing to go against yourself. Who's going to believe in you if you don't believe first?

Remember this: every company needs a CEO. It has to be someone, so why can't it be you, if you believe that you deserve to be the leader? If there is a role in a movie or performance, someone has to play the part; why can't it be you, if you believe that you deserve the role more than anyone else? If there is an award to be given out, someone has to win it; why can't it be you, if you believe that you deserve to win?

What is it that you want in life and what are you prepared to do to get it? Be grateful for all that you have and be interested to learn more. Be mindful of your self-talk, use your imagination, and allow the power of your mind to become your greatest ally. There are millions of opportunities to advance, awards to win, roles to be filled—and it can always be you. In fact, it should be you!

Believe in yourself, become the hero of your own adventure, and maybe someday someone will tell the tale of how you magically transformed pebbles into mountains.

Thank you for reading and I would love to hear your story.

To contact Rich:

Website: www.thepathofme.com

Facebook: www.facebook.com/thepathofme

Twitter: www.twitter.com/thepathofme

LinkedIn: www.linkedin.com/in/richardperrytpom

Telephone: (570)-401-3781

Skype ID: rperry.coaching

Dr. Jin Kyu (Suh) Robertson

Dr. Jin Robertson, a factory girl in Korea, immigrated to America alone at the age twenty-two as a housemaid with little English, a one-way ticket, and a mere $100.

At twenty-eight, Jin, a mother of an eight-month-old baby, joined the U.S. Army as a private to escape from domestic violence. Twenty years later, she retired as a major, and completed her MA (at forty-three) and PhD (at fifty-seven) from Harvard.

As a single mother, she raised her daughter to become a Presidential Scholar (141 of 2.5 million high school graduating seniors selected), a graduate from Harvard (BA) and Princeton (MA), and a U.S. Army officer.

Major Korean TV programs have made documentaries of her dream story that inspired and motivated millions, even saving those on the verge of committing suicides.

She is Korea's most popular inspirational/motivational speaker (over 2,200 speeches), and a best-selling author of the books chronicling her amazing story (over a half million copies sold.) In her American debut memoir, *MAJOR DREAM: From Immigrant Housemaid to Harvard Ph.D.*, she shows readers how to position themselves for a life of success. Discover for yourself why every one of Jin's audiences rises to a rousing standing ovation to this inspiring leader.

My Own Vision, My Own Dream

By Dr. Jin Kyu (Suh) Robertson

To date, I have made many decisions, some of which became major turning points in my life. In turn, these decisions helped me to realize my childhood dreams: becoming an "amhaengosa" (like a Robin Hood, but legal) and a PhD.

The first major change happened when I was twenty-two years old and decided to immigrate to America. I had found a job as a housekeeper for an American family in a Korean newspaper. I knew, as well as everyone else, that it was a dangerous move. In those days, it was common knowledge that many corrupt recruiting agencies would lure innocent girls with lies of respectable work opportunities, and then sell them on the streets of the foreign countries as prostitutes. Everyone I met in Korea seemed to believe that I would succumb to such a fate. I was terrified, naturally. I barely spoke English and had only a one-way ticket and one hundred dollars to my name. Yet, I could not give up. I simply could not deny myself perhaps the only chance to fulfill my dreams. I felt the fear, but did it anyway.

I Saw America!

I was born and raised in Korea. Between World War II and the Korean War, Korea was perhaps the poorest country in the whole world. My life as a girl, growing up in a poor family in a country that discriminated against women and the poor, had been miserable. My desperate dream to become an "amhaengosa" and PhD had been the only light helping me to endure the darkness of the earlier part of my life. Yet, when I ended up working as a wig factory worker, a waitress, and a housekeeper, I began to lose hope for a better future.

That's when I found a newspaper ad looking for a housemaid to work for a family in America—a country I considered paradise. Instantly, I felt a glimmer of hope for my future. "I might be able to realize my childhood dream after all!" Despite the fact that the ad was from a suspicious job agency and that everybody warned me of possibly being sold for prostitution in a foreign country, I took a chance and plunged into the venture head-on.

On March 9, 1971, on a sunny spring day, I boarded the plane, headed to America. All my family and several relatives and friends accompanied me to Gimpo Airport to see me off. Mother looked exhausted from crying since the night before and seemed ready to collapse any minute. Still sobbing, she tightly held on to my hand as if she wouldn't let go of me. I looked around for Father. He was standing alone nearby, but facing away from us. Although I could not see his face, cigarette smoke rising over his thin shoulders said it all. Remembering the night before, I swallowed a lump in my throat.

My last night at home, I came into the room after finishing the dishes and found Father sitting on the floor, smoking. He was always skinny as long as I could remember. But that night, he appeared smaller than before. I sat in front of him and silently watched the white smoke rising to the ceiling like an angel's veil. The familiar cigarette smell teased my nostril as I took a long, deep breath in. To me, it meant my father's smell. I looked around the room as if to etch all the details somewhere in my mind.

'Whenever I missed home, maybe I could pull these images out and stare at them like I am doing now.' I looked at the small entrance door connected to the kitchen that I always hated. It reminded me of many freezing mornings and late nights. The kitchen to me meant discrimination, injustice, anger, and rebellion. Oh, how I wished to move as far away from there as possible. Soon that wish was to be realized.

The Change[5]

After a few minutes, Father pulled out something from his shirt pocket and carefully placed in front of me. It was the first time I saw a hundred-dollar bill.

"I am…sorry I can't give you more…" Father cleared his throat as if something was stuck. "Make sure you eat well…"

Without finishing his words, Father hurried out of the room.

For a long while afterward, I sat there with my head bent and staring at nothing in particular. The hundred-dollar bill that Father left on the floor looked out of place. My parents had no education. They had been working hard all their lives. Yet they were always poor. My parents had to borrow from neighbors to pay the fees for the referral agent and airplane ticket for me.

'At least they just had to pay for a one-way ticket,' I thought.

This was the last time I would see my family for a long while. We said our goodbyes. I turned to walk away, too nervous and excited to allow myself to join in their tears. A few final glances were all I had left to give them.

As I gawked at the foreigners and other well-dressed Koreans in line, I could hear my heartbeat thumping in my ears. My fear rose and dread filled my throat. What if all this was just a part of my imagination? I turned around to have the last look at the road I had left behind. I wondered when and in what state I would return.

Once I was onboard, though, the surroundings made me feel as if I had embarked upon a few days of light travel rather than an enormous life-changing adventure. Scooting into my window seat, I immediately peered out at the airfield. The hundred-dollar bill that Father gave me burned in my pocket. Since my monthly wage in Korea at the time was less than ten dollars, the amount I had was an enormous sum of money. It was, however, not nearly enough to buy a ticket back home. No matter what happened to me in America, I could not return to my home country.

More worries followed one after another. I had no idea what the Korean man looked like who was picking me up at the airport in New York. I knew nothing about him, except things I had heard from his younger brother in Korea. I was not entirely sure if the American family who hired me to be their housemaid would retain me in their employment as two years had passed since they first agreed to employ me. I had no idea if my limited English skills would be enough to help me. The only Americans I knew in the United States were Henry and Wilma, my brief English teachers in Korea. They were now living in San Diego. The only thing I could be sure of at that moment was that I was on a flight to New York.

The plane began to move and gradually picked up speed with every second. Once the airplane took off, my ears deafened and my back was pressed to the seat. The uncomfortable environment inside the plane deepened my sense of isolation from the passengers around me. Despite being cramped, no one seemed to even notice I was there. It frightened me. "Maybe this isn't reality. Maybe I have been pursuing a nightmare instead of a dream."

My ears began to pop. Trying to calm myself, I peeked out the window. I saw the ground below swing back and forth as the plane glided through the air. It seemed an incredible feat to make such a humongous aircraft lift into the air! It was as if the plane weighed no more than a feather! I suppressed my desire to applaud with delight. Gimpo Airport and the surrounding neighborhoods looked surprisingly small. I said goodbye to everything I knew as my life in Korea as the plane rose further into the air. Puffy clouds absorbed the warm sunlight as the world vanished below.

The Change[5]

"This moment is the beginning of achieving a new life. I will return a hero one day. I will prove to all the worth of my dreams," I told myself.

It had been only forty minutes after liftoff, but I felt myself growing tired. I allowed the drowsiness to overtake me, which gradually eased my tense mind.

The plane's startling drop in altitude awakened me. I looked out the window to find only darkness.

When the flight attendants began to distribute meals, I lit up with delight. It was "Western style" food I had rarely had in my life. I emptied my plate with the speed of a famished child.

With a full belly, my mind filled with new hope. I entertained myself during the final hours of the flight by alternating between naps, dreams, and watching the motions of the passengers around me, wondering why they were here and where they were going.

Without warning, I felt a strong push from below as if someone was trying to shoot my body into midair, momentarily leaving me disoriented. I grabbed both armrests as tightly as possible. I wondered if the plane was going to fall from the sky. The deep thump of my heart seemed to pulse audibly. I looked around in confusion. Other passengers seemed unaffected, and calmly straightened their chairs and tightened their seatbelts as the stewardess walked around in haste. I wanted to know what was happening, but calmed down when I realized I was the only one gripped by the unknown. Perhaps we weren't crashing? Had we had finally arrived in America?

Moments later, I could see Chicago just out my window. It looked so peaceful that my fear began to subside. I was glad I had come. The gigantic plane descended gracefully to the runway below and rolled to a stop at the terminal gateway. The first stop on my path to freedom!

"We thank you for flying Delta Airlines and hope you had a pleasant trip." As if someone had heard my silent question, the intercom squawked in Korean after the English announcement.

Passengers around me began to quickly gather their belongings. I went through my mental checklist of documents needed to pass through customs. It had taken two years to receive my immigrant visa. Those documents were more precious than gold; they were my ticket to "Freedom and Success."

As we exited the plane, I pulled my tuberculosis chest x-ray down from the overhead compartment. It was in a large brown envelope, precisely as long as my upper torso. Standing tall, holding it with both hands in front of my chest, I felt like I was carrying a banner proudly declaring my first trip to America.

The US Government wasn't about to let immigrants into the United States without medical release forms and chest x-rays. Tuberculosis was rampant in Korea at the time. All Koreans heading to America for the first time held these "tickets to freedom" safely in our hands. Those Koreans without these documents and x-rays smiled kindly, probably remembering their first journey to the United States.

I can't honestly remember the back corridors of Chicago's immigration. With almost no English, I somehow passed through the INS system receiving my first thumping stamp of approval before being put back on another plane bound for New York. My life in a new world was now only hours away.

After the long journey from Korea to Chicago, the connecting flight to New York was easier. I settled into my chair, shifting gently until I found the sweet spot of comfort like the passengers around me.

The Change[5]

The altitude change made my eyelids heavy once again. Neither the chilly cabin air filled my lungs, nor could my excitement keep me from falling asleep. My eyes fluttered shut into the heaviness of dream.

"Burr, it's so cold here."

I was once again by the side of the river with a mountain of laundry. It was winter, and the water was frozen as solid as a rock. I tried to crack the ice with a sharp stone, but to no avail. My fingers and toes began to numb and the laundry pile seemed to get bigger by the minute. The sky grew dark and there came the howling of wild dogs. I wanted to get home, but couldn't find it. I was dragging the dirty laundry and wandered aimlessly in search of my house.

"Where is everyone? I don't know where I am. Help…" I tried to yell, but there was only a small whisper.

Then I heard a soft voice. "Jin, you can make it on your own; just believe in yourself!"

"Who are you? What do you mean?"

"Just do what your heart tells you. You will be fine."

"Wait! Tell me who you are…"

But it was too late, the voice didn't answer. Then out of nowhere, there came a bright light. The surroundings became bright all around. My heart felt light, and my feet seemed to fly in the air, higher and higher.

"Why this must be…"

"Garble, garble…New York…garble."

I was awakened by a loud voice in the most incomprehensible language. Then I heard "New York" among a cluster of words. When I opened my eyes, I found myself facing the window. The warm sunlight was streaming through as the ocean below shimmered happily.

'Where am I?'

I looked around in confusion. Then suddenly, I felt a strong push from below as if someone were trying to shoot my body into midair.

'Oh my God…I am on a plane!'

In panic, I grabbed both armrests as tightly as possible. I was sure the plane was going to fall off the sky. Once again, the other passengers seemed emotionless. I wanted to know what was happening but decided not to ask any questions. I simply copied them.

'Maybe…we have finally arrived in New York?' Suddenly, my heart began to race faster and louder. 'Oh, I hope…'

"Ladies and gentlemen, we will be landing in New York in ten minutes. Please buckle your seatbelts. We hope that…" At last!

The plane began to descend toward my final destination.

'So this is America. It seems so peaceful from up here…I'm glad I came.'

The plane slowly descended…and landed gracefully.

I gathered my luggage and headed toward the exit. While I was walking, I remembered my dreams. Then it occurred to me that the voice was none other than my own. As I was thinking of this dream, I saw another one. A dream of a world that was just and free. I saw a dream of a world of opportunity. Then I saw the dream come true in front of my very own eyes.

I saw America.

That's how my life in America began forty-four years ago.

God must have been watching over that scared but brave and hopeful girl! I did not get sold on the street as a prostitute. I did not even work as a housemaid. Because it took two years for my visa to get through, the job was gone to a Hispanic woman by the time I reached the home of my American sponsor. Though I panicked initially, I later realized it was "a blessing in disguise." In less than two years, I was a college student by day and a waitress at a high-class Korean restaurant by night. I felt like I was on top of the world.

Yet, in 1976, I had to make another major life change—I joined the U.S. Army. I was the mother of an eight-month-old baby girl and a battered wife. It took every fiber of my being to resist the urge to kill the abuser as revenge. To keep myself from becoming a murderer, I became a licensed warrior instead. The Army became my refuge from domestic violence.

As well as being a major turning point in my life, joining the Army was also a "blessing in disguise." The U.S. Army took a twenty-eight-year-old broken-down private and allowed her to soar like an eagle. Twenty years later, I retired as a major with a master's degree from Harvard. By then, I also spoke fluent English and Japanese, in addition to my native language, Korean. The army also allowed me to finish Harvard PhD, my childhood dream!

My daughter, Jasmin Cho, said that her childhood dream was becoming her mother's clone! Following in my footstep, she graduated from Harvard, served in the U.S. Army, and speaks three languages (English, Korean, and Japanese) fluently.

While I was pursuing my PhD, a Korean TV program decided to make a documentary film of my life story. This program was the catalyst to my writing my life story, which became the number one best-selling book in Korea, inspiring, motivating, and empowering millions of Koreans. These events led me to discover a talent and passion I did not know I possessed—motivational speaking. I soon found myself traveling throughout the world as an inspirational speaker.

I am so thankful that I did not run away from all the tough obstacles in my life. I am so glad that I did not succumb to my fears, but took on the challenges head-on. I am overjoyed that my stories of trials and triumphs are helping billions of people who desire to better their lives. Most of all, I am so grateful that God gave me such a wonderful opportunity called life.

To contact Jin:

Email: jin@drjinrobertson.com

Websites: http://www.drjinrobertson.com and http://cafe.daum.net/ilovecon

In USA: Ms. Jasmin Cho Abel; Tel: 1-917-881-7406; jas1cho@hotmail.com

In Korea: Ms. Inchon Suh; Tel: +82-10-3685-4632 (in Korea: 010-3685-4632); suhinchon@hanmail.net

Leonie Newton

Leonie Newton is an innovator, educator, and entrepreneur. Compassion, open-mindedness, and contributing to the improvement of the environment, herself, and others are Leonie's drivers.

Before turning to Life Coaching, Leonie's teaching career flourished until a work-related mental breakdown created an urgent need for change. Traditional Western medicine and psychology did little to aid her recovery, compelling Leonie to search further afield.

Studying Neuro-Linguistic Programming (NLP), Deep State Re-Patterning, EDISC Behavior Profiling, Strategic Intervention and Mindfulness (to name a few) provided the tools and insights Leonie needed to not only recover from the work injury, but also ensured she never again experience the depression or anxiety related to significant traumas from earlier in her life. Having invested almost $100,000 in her education, Leonie believes that putting into action everything learned is a guarantee for success.

Leonie now utilizes her eclectic skill set, strategies, and real-life experiences to transform others' lives, literally all over the world. Leonie's coaching career began with the intention of focusing on assisting teachers and students (which continues to be a passion), yet Leonie's own life experience attracts clients needing to shift personal barriers to success, including Post Traumatic Stress Disorder, depression, and anxiety. Additionally, Leonie also mentors other Life Coaches with all levels of experience including those just starting on their new journey.

From Self-Loathing to Self-Loving

By Leonie Newton

Imagine yourself dehydrated, exhausted, and frantic at the edge of a foreboding, unexplored, dense forest. In the distance, you hear the promise of cool, refreshing water flowing. Desperate to survive, what do you do? Logically, you forge the fastest path possible to the source of your survival, despite your fears. You battle your way through the unrelenting scrub knowing that turning back is not an option, regardless of the unknown perils that lay ahead. With the sound of your nourishing life source in the distance as your only guide, wearily you press on. Large boulders and sheer drops along the way force you to divert from your original bearings and eventually, exhausted and parched, you are successful in your endeavor to reach your destination.

The effort required was considerable and the water is not as pleasant as you dreamed. In fact, it's rancid and makes you feel ill. Disappointed, you resign yourself to the fact that this is your only option and as good as it gets. The beaten trail awaits you to effortlessly follow it whenever you find yourself at the edge of that forest again in need of nourishing. It defies logic to even consider finding a different route, knowing the immense energy spent on creating the original that you depend on for survival.

Imagine now, years later, you fly over the forest with your well-worn path clearly visible from a bird's-eye view. To your dismay, you realize how clumsy and dangerous it is. As well-trodden and familiar as it is, from your newly elevated position, you become aware of a shortcut that leads to a significantly cleaner, faster-flowing water supply that would have quenched your thirst and sustained you significantly more from the start.

If only you knew there was a better way to begin with, logically you would have saved yourself repeated, arduous trips to the same, polluted destination. The result could have been a vastly healthier and happier outcome.

Realize now, this process happens millions of times a day and takes less than a millisecond to accomplish in real time. Our brains do this by firing neural pathways each time we experience something new. When we must make a decision, rather than trekking into unfamiliar territory, we follow the course of action we are most familiar with, even when the outcomes aren't necessarily desirable.

We assign a meaning to this path and this meaning becomes a *belief*, which we continue to gather data to support. We begin to live as though this belief is the only one possible, so we repeat patterns of behavior to support it, which can be destructive or *limiting*.

Adding to our limiting beliefs are our choices of where to place ownership on events, actions, or thoughts. When we believe that things happen to us because of others' actions, we will always be at the mercy of others. This is living *at effect,* which deletes our power to change situations. Alternatively, when we choose to own that everything in our lives is caused by our own choices either directly or indirectly, we are living *at cause,* which is the only way to have the power to change our lives. This can be a challenging concept for some to grasp in the early stages of self-empowerment. There are certain situations where it seems impossible for us to have control at all, such as in the case of car accidents and other tragedies. However, if you want to create positive change in your life, it is imperative that you embrace this notion, as it will determine your level and speed of success or not. It is only once we genuinely acknowledge the role *we* play in our experiences that we can start to shift our *limiting beliefs* and ultimately, the quality and outcomes of our experiences.

Remember, many people live with the misconception that our experiences determine our beliefs. Reality is the other way around. We filter our experiences to *match* our beliefs by deleting, distorting, and generalizing all other evidence that might prove our beliefs wrong.

What does any of this have to do with self-loathing or self-loving? My story begins with living at effect and ends with living at cause.

As far as most people could tell, I was an intelligent, friendly, and social lady in her late thirties, who was successful at work and now happily married with three great children.

Even my closest family and friends never knew the extent of my self-loathing and despair. They could clearly see positive things about me that I ignored. My limiting beliefs began at such a young age that by the age of twelve, I couldn't believe one positive thing about myself. I perfected my self-loathing stories in my mind so well that I continued to have experiences to match.

At merely eighteen months old, I made decisions about men, pain, fear, and my place in the world. My godfather had a son roughly my age. The boy was crying on the floor after a failed attempt to climb down steps. I looked down at him from the same step he had just fallen from as my godfather entered the room. I vividly recall the anger on his face as he concluded that this was my doing and oh boy, was I in trouble! With boots on, my godfather kicked me. Terrified and in incredible pain, even at 18 months old, I gave this experience a meaning.

It was over thirty years before I understood the full impact of how this and related, subsequent events contributed to my life of self-loathing and self-destructive behaviors. This was the first time I stood at the edge of the forest and beat the path that would repeatedly bring me back to the same undesirable outcomes.

The meanings or limiting beliefs I assigned to that event were: Men were to be feared; I was powerless to stop them; Life is unfair.

I am the youngest of three girls and my parents remained married until the death of my father eleven years ago. They worked and were upstanding citizens of the community, yet had a limited social life. They were very loving and provided well for us, despite their authoritarian approach to parenting. My sisters were only eighteen months apart in age, well liked, possessed fantastic social lives, and even shared mutual friends.

At three and four years younger than my sisters and physically incapable of doing the things they did, I was just a pain to them, the annoying little sister, just like millions of younger siblings around the world. I reduced my loneliness by spending every minute I could with my father in his shed, seeking his approval, getting as greasy as possible. If he had a spot of dirt on his hands, I would grab the messiest car part I could and smother my hands in grease. It was sure to impress him. My fear of men included my father, but not to the same degree as others. He had hard, calloused hands that hurt like hell when we copped a wallop from him and we avoided angering him. His temper was short and fiery and he was incredibly opinionated, but we knew he loved us. I idolized him, did my best to be just like him, and essentially, I was successful.

So, if I had such a 'normal' upbringing in a loving household, with two emotionally stable sisters, how did I become so self-loathing?

School was perfect for gathering data that proved I didn't belong. I already believed I didn't fit in with my own family and I dragged this belief through to interactions with my peers. Most of my school years were spent alone or drifting between groups of friends. I learned quickly to move on to the next group before my welcome wore out.

If you said my appearance was hideous at the age of five, I would have agreed wholeheartedly. My straggly, limp brown hair was rarely brushed properly and usually looked like a bird's nest. My pasty skin wasn't smoothly tanned; it was freckly like I had mud splattered all over me, which in later years resulted in my nickname of "fly-shit face." What a lovely name for a little girl! My nose was perpetually blistered, red, and peeling from sunburn after refusing to wear a hat or sunblock. My body was short, stocky, and disproportionately heavyset in my legs, which was far from appealing compared to the slim, tall, tanned girls. These physical features won't get you into the popular groups. It didn't help that I was deaf in my left ear and misheard questions, which I then answered completely inappropriately, adding further embarrassment to my pitiful existence.

Mine was a very lonely and humiliating existence. My most challenging relationships were with girls. After spending so much time in the company of an adult male, I simply didn't know how to relate to them. Mood swings and bitchiness were unfamiliar to me and I wasn't interested in becoming comfortable with them either. Boys were easier.

I'm certain many of you can relate to what I call "small town syndrome." In a small town, it doesn't matter what you do (or don't do), stories are created for a bit of excitement. The stories about me were wild, hurtful, and inaccurate, most of the time. Twice during primary school, I had boyfriends who I felt at ease and complete with. I dare say I even felt happy with them. On both occasions, our relationships ended when their families left the region. Life was unfair. I was only a young girl and had never even kissed a boy, but that didn't stop the stories stating otherwise from spreading like wildfire. I hated girls. I believed they were mean, selfish, and liars. I repeatedly found evidence to prove my beliefs about them to be true. Boys were easier.

The Change[5]

At the age of twelve, during my first year of high school, I had my first sexual encounter, with an eighteen-year-old man. He was the older brother of a boy from school. I had no idea of their intentions when they invited me to go fishing. Due to having so few friends and being desperate to fit in anywhere, when the older brother offered alcohol, I couldn't refuse in case they turned me away. The stories they heard about me piqued their interest. In no time, I was drunk and raped.

Men were to be feared; I was powerless to stop them; Life was unfair.

My embarrassment and guilt was so overwhelming that I considered ending my life in preference to shaming my parents and sisters with what *I* had done. I despised myself almost as much as I hated the rest of the insidious world. With my victim mentality and constant dwelling on the unfairness of life, my evidence gathering gained momentum as my negative beliefs repeatedly proved accurate.

For over thirty years, I consistently gathered evidence, from mean girls at school and boys who got angry when I said "no" to sex, to controlling and violent relationships, which escalated into several near-death experiences at the hands of my partners. My fear of men grew to the point where I was so terrified of what they would do to me if fought back that I would freeze, which they took full advantage of. One of the seven rapes I endured resulted in a pregnancy, which I aborted. I couldn't bear the thought of that vile, evil thing growing inside me. Every day for over 30 years, I harbored immense guilt, shame, and remorse for my choice. I was so young I didn't know what else to do. This remorse intensified years later when I was told I could never have children because of damage I received during one of the violent attacks. Two other rapes were due to drink spiking. One of which happened during my marriage. I didn't tell my husband for over a year I was so ashamed I had let it happen. Apart from the men involved, nobody—not even my family—knew. I was so ashamed of my despicable existence that I never wanted anyone to know. I became incredibly creative with the truth in an attempt to hide each situation as it arose, adding further to my shame. As far as I was concerned, I was nothing but a dirty, worthless, completely miserable and pathetic liar, a waste of oxygen.

Between twelve and thirty-eight, I attempted suicide six times. Subconsciously though, as much as I wanted to die, I knew if I took my life, I would simply transfer the pain to my family. I guess this is why I failed, fortunately, each time. I had already brought enough shame, heartache, and embarrassment to them as it was, although thankfully, they were unaware.

My beliefs continued driving me into situations where I could continue to gather supporting evidence. The pinnacle of this was a work-related, mental breakdown, which landed me bed bound, mute, and sedated for three weeks and took eight months to recover from. As much as I wanted to talk, especially to my children and husband, my brain had shut down and my mental and physical capabilities were overrun by uncontrollable emotions. Psychology and medication only marginally helped. After four months of weekly therapy, the psychiatrist's report to my workplace dealt the final blow. It stated it would be a minimum of two years before I would be capable of returning to work and even then, only to light duties.

I sunk to the lowest point of my doleful life, realizing I was to be a burden on my husband and children for at least two years. This was exactly what I needed to hear. It pushed me to the point where my reasons for changing were so enormous that there was no option but to change for the better and fast. I read his words and immediately set out to prove him wrong.

My self-loving began in that moment and Life followed suit. I finally *believed* I deserved better than this and so did my family. As a young girl, I was fascinated with my mother's collection of personal empowerment books. At nineteen, I discovered Anthony Robbins' audiotapes; however, I never put into practice what I learned.

Now I was motivated and ready to own the peaceful, happy life offered in those valuable resources. I enrolled in a Diploma of Life Coaching, whilst still teaching. I had already studied various strands of psychology and human social behavior, and embedded them in my teaching practice with phenomenal results for my students over the previous ten years. I read, re-read, listened to, and watched everything I possibly could via books, DVDs, and the Internet. I enrolled in course after course on self-empowerment. I had the tools I needed. I used them every minute of every day that I possibly could.

After a few months of daily meditation and consistent goal setting, followed by the actions to match, I had significantly changed my brain chemistry to the point where my medication was now creating more problems than it solved. It took only two months to completely stop all antidepressant and antianxiety medication I had taken for the previous six months. My doctor supported my every step and was amazed at how quickly my mental and physical health improved.

During my self-managed healing process, multiple, extremely traumatic situations occurred involving my closest family members. My doctor revealed to me some time later how she expected me to fall back into a state of psychosis again, as they were such significant events that even the most stable person would have struggled to deal with the stress of them. Her acknowledgement of my success was so empowering that I knew I had to share my knowledge to help others. I returned to full-time work one and a half years earlier than predicted, then resigned to begin life coaching full time.

Every day, I am extremely grateful for each event that brought me to now and I appreciate everything in life, especially myself. My experiences enable me to help others turn their lives around because I know what it is like to be at the bottom of the deepest, darkest pit of depression, anxiety, shame, guilt, and self-loathing. And I know how to not only climb out of that pit, but to keep on reaching previously unimaginable heights of success, inner-peace, meaningful connection with others, and self-love.

Two of the most significant understandings I needed to embrace were:

1. *Every person is simply doing the best they can with the tools they have, in that moment. If they knew a better way, they would choose it!*

This applies to every human being, myself included. It released me of the anger, hatred, guilt, and loathing I had bound in my head and heart towards the men who raped or abused me, the school bullies, and mostly, myself for my part in repeatedly making the same mistakes that ended in violence and self-loathing. If those people knew a better way to gain what they were ultimately searching for, they would have chosen it. If I knew a better way to gain the needs of belonging, love, connection, and significance I desperately searched for, I can assure you I would have chosen that instead. I could finally acknowledge that I was not a bad person who deserved bad experiences. I was just a human being at the edge of the self-loathing forest, following the same path to the same un-resourceful outcome. Once I had new knowledge and knew that Life would be better, it was. It is that simple because I just had to keep on taking steps towards my desired outcomes.

2. *It is only my response to situations and people that determines whether they are stressful or not, because every event is external to me.*

I now *know* that people and situations have no power over my emotions—only I do. If want to take on sadness, fear, or anger when a person speaks or acts, that is my choice, just as I could choose happiness, laughter, and other meanings. Other people are *not* responsible for reactions within me; *I am* one hundred percent responsible for choosing how or even *if* I respond. This is such a powerful realization because it made me aware of my repeated patterns. I relied so heavily on others to make me feel good or happy that I never bothered to do it for myself. The day I had this "Aha" moment, my husband was released from the impossible, endless task of being my source amusement and now he can just relax and be my friend who I share laughs and quality time with when it suits us both.

These two understandings changed my life because I allowed them to. No one and nothing will ever get me to choose self-loathing over self-loving again.

When you reach your point where change is the only option, connect with me and let's see just how high you can climb out of the self-loathing pit you've been living in.

To Contact Leonie:

Telephone: (Australia Mobile) +61402269049

Website: www.opportunemoments.com.au

Facebook: Opportune Moments Success Coaching

Skype: leonie.omsc

Kay R. Sanders

Kay Sanders is a Certified Holistic Life & Sales Coach who draws from her own experiences and struggles in life and in sales to inspire others and to make a difference in their life. She was born and raised in Germany and came to the U.S. with the desire of achieving big things in life. Her passion and dedication to fulfill her life purpose was helping her to overcome all the roadblocks that kept getting in her way, trying to keep her from accomplishing what she had set out to do. In the process, she found her passion for personal development and success and discovered the way to change her beliefs, her mind-set, and her actions, which guided her and allowed her to become the great coach she is today.

Kay has guided her clients to personal mastery and success. Through her teaching and coaching, her clients were able to make major positive changes—both professionally and personally. She works with clients to clarify their goals and visions, identifying key strategic milestone objectives, uncover hidden challenges and blind spots that could be sabotaging their success, and creating a long-term plan and a next step action plan.

Kay brings a wide range of experience and education to the table which her clients can benefit from. She is the author of the book *The Coaching Business Blueprint,* which teaches the ins and outs of starting, running, and growing a professional coaching business. She also has created a Sales Acceleration Training Program that teaches the proper sales process, which will assist individuals in the sales industry to become a master in sales.

Kay truly believes that everyone not only deserves, but also has the ability, to live a fulfilling life full of success and achievements.

The Power of the Mind

By Kay R. Sanders

Have you ever wondered why the things you wish for simply don't come true? Have you wished for a better job or to meet Mr. or Mrs. Right, but instead you are still stuck with a job you are not very happy with and every guy or female you meet turns out to be far from what you wanted? Does this sound familiar? One possible explanation for this problem could be that your mind-set is getting in the way of your getting the things you want in just the way you want them. The mind is a very powerful tool that can either push or guide us to become successful or hold us back.

I had never really thought about how much my mind could affect my life until a few years ago when I was reading the book *You Become What You Think About* by Vic Johnson. It was really an eye-opener since it became clear to me how much I had been hurting myself because of my negative and limiting mind-set. After reading this book, I did some soul searching and discovered the origin of some of my limiting beliefs and how they had been affecting my life.

When I first started in network marketing many years ago, I always thought, "They are not going to spend their hard-earned money on this!" And that's exactly what had happened. I became quite frustrated because I never was able to make a sale. Even though at first I thought it was because of the products, in fact it was my mind-set that was holding me back because I always felt pushy and uncomfortable asking for the money. Being in sales, however, was not the only area of my life that was affected by my limiting mind-set. Other areas, such as my health and relationships, were affected as well. It took me many years to realize that all this time I was sabotaging myself, causing me to be unhappy and miserable. Once I learned about the Law of Belief, my life turned around, and I became much happier. I finally started attracting the things I wanted, and I was able to achieve one goal after another.

The Law of Belief

The Law of Belief is best explained by the following: "What we believe becomes reality." Once we change the way we think about how we act and the world around us, we can change our reality and also our own performance. The Law of Belief is the key to happiness and success. Once we truly believe that we can become successful and accomplish what we want or have anything we want, we will have it in just that way. But if we don't truly believe, then we hold ourselves back and don't achieve what we want to achieve.

"It is not until you believe it that you will see it."

How many times have you wanted something, but it simply did not happen for you? It is our limiting beliefs that keep us from getting the things we want in just the way we want them. You may want to have something or have it in a certain way, but deep down, you don't truly believe that you can attain it.

Henry Ford once said: "Whether you think you can or whether you think you can't, you're right."

In order for the Law of Belief to be effective, you must first know exactly what it is that you want in exactly the way you want it. Once you have a crystal-clear picture of what you want and truly believe that you can and will have it in just that way, you will slowly but surely manifest the things you truly want. But you must believe!

Many who try to apply the Law of Belief fail or give up too soon because just like everything else in life, things take time. If you don't continually reinforce your beliefs, you might end up giving up too soon. Being consistent and maintaining focus on your goals is possibly the greatest challenge you have to face.

You have to maintain your faith and belief that things will change and that you will accomplish what you have set out to do, even though setbacks and roadblocks are trying to prevent you from accomplishing your goals. The path to success and happiness is not always easy, but even obstacles can be seen as something positive because we can learn from our setbacks, and they allow us to grow as a person. If you look back and think about all the obstacles you have had to face throughout your life, were they all truly bad, or did you learn from them, and did they help you make better choices the next time you faced the same obstacle? Such obstacles make us who we are today. They help us grow as a person, and they guide us to make better decisions later in life. I believe that everything happens for a reason and that no matter what we have to go through in life, we all have a choice to continue moving forward or giving up at the first sign of trouble. If we choose to give up, we can never hope to reach our goals, but once we learn to persevere, we eventually create the reality we truly deserve.

In order to make the Law of Belief work in your favor, you must begin to believe. You must clearly understand what it is that you want to achieve and then decide what you have to do to accomplish your goals. You need to get into the habit of acting as if you had already accomplished these goals.

Our behavior influences our beliefs, and it helps manifest our desire, and all personal breakthroughs begin with a change in beliefs.

Beliefs

Our beliefs are formed by what we learned from our parents and what we have learned through personal experiences. They even include things we have learned from others, and those beliefs become part of our identity. They can either help us move forward or they can hold us back from seeing and fulfilling our true potential. We all have our own concept of the world. Your concept of the world, for example, is different from mine, but we all know how we see things and the way we feel about things. Every day, we are being influenced by different entities, such as the media, friends, family, and even coworkers or strangers you meet in a coffee shop. We form our beliefs from what influences us, but it is up to each one of us to decide what beliefs we keep and what beliefs we allow to influence our every move. Our strongly held beliefs drive us to take action, and you have to choose the beliefs that challenge you and move you forward instead of holding you back.

All beliefs, whether they are positive or negative, exist for a reason. Some act as comfortable protective armor because they protect us from getting hurt. For example, let's say you have always had bad luck regarding relationships. Every guy you have met cheated on you, always lied to you, and maybe even treated you badly. Because of those experiences, you developed a negative mind-set concerning relationships, and it might be something like the following: "Every guy I meet turns out to be a loser. They all lie and cheat on me. No guy ever treats me right." Such thinking will keep you from ever meeting the right guy because you have already decided that the next guy you meet will be just like all these other guys. Even though such negative thinking will sabotage you from meeting the guy of your dreams, it also acts as a protective barrier because you already expect that something bad will happen. Accordingly, you won't allow yourself to let your guard down because the guy might not be the type of guy you expect. All these negative thoughts or beliefs take root on a subconscious level, and most people use limiting beliefs because it keeps them safe in their comfort zone. We have all done it!

Our actions today are influenced by interpretations we have made in the past, both positive and negative. Our most limiting beliefs about ourselves may get in the way of any actions we need to take to move forward and accomplish what we want to achieve. If we believe we are not smart enough to get that job we want so badly or that we are not pretty enough to meet our soul mate, then we basically give ourselves permission to not even try. If we believe that all men or women we meet or date are cheaters, liars, and simply no good, we will end up building that protective barrier around ourselves to protect us from getting hurt. Such limits may protect us, but in reality they are very limiting because they keep us from ever being in a happy relationship.

Anthony Robbins said: "Beliefs have the power to create and the power to destroy."

Our beliefs are what determine our life and the things we want. They create that reality. Who we are is based on our beliefs, and they determine our behavior, our feelings, and our thoughts.

The Subconscious Mind

The way our mind works is pretty simple. It consists of two parts: the conscious mind and the subconscious mind. Think of it as an iceberg where the top 10 percent that you see above the water is your conscious mind. The other 90 percent of the iceberg that's beneath the water, the part you can't see, is your subconscious mind. So which part do you think really drives our behavior? The subconscious. We all have certain beliefs about ourselves on a subconscious level that prevent us from achieving our potential. Any negative beliefs you have about yourself or your abilities act as an anchor that is holding you back from achieving certain things in life.

Our actions are controlled by our subconscious mind, and if our conscious mind is not in harmony with our belief system or our subconscious mind, our actions will not produce any results. The purpose of the subconscious mind is to keep us consistent with our identity and how we describe ourselves to others.

"We become what we say. We become our self-image, matching to our self-belief."

Negative/Limiting Beliefs

The mind is a very interesting entity and easily influenced. Did you know that we hurt ourselves just by our thoughts? Have you ever had a situation where on a subconscious level, not knowing that you are doing it, you talk yourself into having the worse pain ever or where you talk yourself into being too afraid of something that you decide not to do it after all? Our brain believes what we tell it. If we think pain, we get pain; if we think fear, we get fear. The root cause of limiting beliefs stems from a fear of failure or fear of rejection. You might wish for a better position where you are employed, but deep down you might fear that you won't live up to the expectations that come with the position. This type of limiting belief was formed with positive intentions to protect you from the pain that would come from failure and not being able to live up to expectations and perhaps even being fired. All our mind is trying to do is protect us from the pain and agony that come with failure, disappointment, or rejection.

Everything starts with a thought, and if we think bad thoughts, bad things happen, but if we think good thoughts, good things happen.

"Things only have the meaning that we give them."

Positive Self Talk—Affirmations

We have around 50,000 thoughts every day, and 95 percent of these are repeated daily. One way to reprogram the subconscious mind is through autosuggestion, which means that you repeat to yourself the same thing over and over and over again. Change begins with language, and there is a vocabulary to success.

Affirmations are a powerful tool that you can use to reprogram your subconscious mind and influence your life. Affirmations are positive statements that are repeated out loud to change your beliefs, habits, and thought patterns. Through repetition, the subconscious mind accepts the affirmation, and the statement becomes part of your way of thinking. The subconscious mind is the root of our issues; if you have limiting beliefs, they are embedded deep in your subconscious mind. By using affirmation frames, you can free your subconscious mind and eliminate these beliefs.

Through affirmation frames, you can achieve excellence through motivation. You will approach your life with a passion, drive, energy, and motivation to make the most of everything and achieve success. You are able to increase your desires and level of ambition to fuel your motivation, instead of settling for second best. You will be able to take more action instead of procrastinating. And most of all, you will be able to change the way your mind works and start enjoying getting things done and the reward that comes with being highly motivated.

A positive affirmation is simply a statement that affirms something is true. Through repetition and consistency, the statement becomes stored in your mind and starts changing your beliefs. It influences your personality and even alters your behavior. For example, if you say such phrases as "I can do anything I put my mind to" or "I am a master in sales" and say such phrases over and over again, eventually you will start to really believe it, and it will influence your personality. Most of all, you will become more confident.

Consistency is the key to using affirmation to change your way of thinking. As you know, change doesn't happen overnight, and even though affirmation frames are very powerful, they do take time to have a positive effect. Make a commitment to recite your affirmations every day, three times a day—it's best to do this in the morning, during the day, and in the evening. Say your affirmations out loud ten times each day and you will quickly notice a difference. You could even record yourself saying the affirmations and listen to it three times a day or at night. If the noise doesn't bother you, you could let the recording play throughout the night.

"Change begins in language, and when you change your language, you can change your reality."

I am about to share with you some affirmation phrases that I use myself and that you can use if you feel you are holding yourself back because you fear failure.

I will achieve great things

I am capable of massive success

I stay positive at all times

I stay persistent until I achieve success

I persist despite any setbacks

I go all out to achieve my goals

Nothing is stopping me from accomplishing my goals

I put full effort into any tasks I start

Success comes naturally to me

I always pursue my dreams

I will achieve my ultimate potential in life

I only think positively about myself and my ambitions

I make a difference in the world

I have everything I need to become successful

Just as positive affirmations change our behavior and beliefs, negative thoughts or limiting beliefs do the same. Examples of such limiting beliefs could be that "I'm not experienced enough," "I'm not good enough," "I don't have it in me," "I don't have a college degree," "I'm too old," "I don't have any money," "I'm too afraid," "I don't have the time." If we focus on such limiting beliefs, they will end up holding us back because our subconscious mind adapts to what we say to ourselves, which results in holding ourselves back and limiting ourselves from accomplishing great things.

Affirmation, Visualization, and The Law of Attraction go hand in hand because the way we think or the things we think about also applies to the things we have in life. We attract the things we focus on the most. Unfortunately, most people focus on what they don't want instead of focusing on the things they do want. For example, if you want to become successful with your business or your sales career, focus on that. See it as if it has already happened. Imagine how it will feel when you are successful. The same thing applies if you are currently renting and your dream is to own your own home. Draw a mental picture of having that—your dream home. Picture it exactly the way you want it. By focusing on what you want, you basically think it into existence—your subconscious mind always catches up with what we think about, so if you think big, you will get big. If you think successful, you will become successful, but if you keep focusing on negative things and think you will never be able to make it in sales or that you will never be able to own your dream home, guess what's going to happen—nothing! Nothing is going to happen because you don't allow yourself to let it happen.

Having the proper mind-set where your beliefs are in sync with your conscious mind is especially important and affects many different aspects in life, including happiness, success, relationships, career, health, and even finances. If you truly want to live a more fulfilling life and accomplish anything you want, you must change your mind-set and truly believe in yourself and that you deserve to have whatever it is you desire in just the way you want it. Doing this is the key to lifelong success and happiness.

I believe that the universe rewards those who think big and take action differently from those who don't.

To contact Kay:

Kay Sanders Coaching

Founder and Creator of Kay Sanders Coaching, Embracing Sales, and UrOneStop Desktop Publishing Services

Direct: 915.216.2743

E-mail: kay@kaysanders.com

Websites: www.kaysanders.com, www.embracingsales.com, www.uronestop.com

To schedule an appointment with Kay:
http://bit.ly/CoachingInquiry

Reginald F. Butler

Reginald is the founder and CEO of Performance Paradigm, an executive education, human capital consultancy.

He is a highly recognized motivational speaker and corporate consultant/educator with over 28 years of experience in delivering transformative learning solutions within the private, corporate, and non-profit sectors. He is recognized and sought after for his unique delivery of high-energy motivational messages for personal, professional, team, and organizational improvement. He motivates his audiences by utilizing an experiential learning methodology and leverages behavioral modification techniques to deliver his unique and transformative sessions. He consistently leaves his audiences with incredible insights for personal growth and enhanced organizational effectiveness.

Working within both the Fortune 1000 and the non-profit sector, he serves a wide portfolio of diverse clients and industries both domestically and abroad. He has delivered his dynamic experiences to clients such as PwC, Goldman Sachs, Capital One, Proctor and Gamble, SC Johnson, Walmart, Limited Brands, Luxottica Brands, Novartis, Cardinal Health, St. Louis Children's Hospital, Tampa General Hospital, Black Entertainment Television, Gulf Power, Mississippi Power, Marriott International, NABA, ALPFA, Brigham Young University, Howard University, Lehigh University, and NYU-Stern School of Business.

His areas of expertise include high performing team development, organizational change management, diversity and inclusion, executive leadership development, conflict resolution, trainer development, workforce retention strategies, and executive coaching.

Reginald holds a Masters in Educational Administration from Xavier University in Cincinnati and received his undergraduate degree in theatre and music from Washington University in St. Louis.

Director's Cut: The Adaptive Mind-set

By Reginald F. Butler

"You can't change behaviors without first changing the mind-set through which you view the world. Period."

Reginald Butler

Founder of Performance Paradigm LLC

"You want to know why I'm so upset? It's because of how he talked to me. 'I'm pleasantly surprised you made it. Congratulations!' That's exactly what he said to me. Can you believe it, what was he expecting? I've been working my tail off to advance here. I've had nothing but great evaluations since I started. I've even outperformed the revenue targets for my team two years in a row! And he's 'pleasantly surprised'. Seriously? I've got too much going on in my life to let him bring me down."

Um, wow. As her coach I just had to ask—"Have you considered he possibly meant that as a compliment?"

A considerable amount of time elapsed before Jennifer answered.

"You're kidding right? He knew exactly what he was doing. He was letting me know I couldn't make it around here without him. He was keeping me in my place. Do you know what I'm dealing with? Both of my kids are in college. One of them was just in a fender bender. I'm in the middle of negotiations on buying a home so I can be closer to the office. And I still have to sell my current house. Replace the air conditioner, fix the roof, 'stage the house,' so no one can tell the ethnicity of who lives there—really? My agent actually had me take down most of my family pictures. Said the potential buyers had to be able to 'see themselves' on the walls, not someone else because it may bias their decision."

And we have made a left turn onto Off Topic Street. Let's get back on track. "Could it have been a compliment?" I asked again.

"My agent hasn't given me a compliment since we met. I'm thinking about firing him."

Oh boy. "Jennifer, your manager, could it have been a compliment? Could it have actually been congratulatory?"

"Well if it was, it was certainly a strange way to congratulate someone."

Her eye contact became erratic and her tone of voice and pace changed ever so slightly.

"This is too much for me. It's like I'm in a bad movie. There are way too many moving pieces to manage at the same time. I feel like I need a change if I'm going to survive all of this."

Well now we're getting somewhere. "Change can be good," I told her, "but only if you're ready to accept certain things. Some change will be about your environment or other people, and some change will be about you. Most importantly, you have to be willing to move forward. Are you ready?"

"May I have some water?"

Scene.

The above scene is a snippet of how I spend my days as a leadership consultant and coach. As I work to do my part and help others with changes they need to make in their lives, I sometimes wonder how it's possible to filter through the noise of life to identify the things that may be holding us back. We all must navigate the digital sound bites of headlines ranging from civil protest that conjure the 1960s to parents being arrested for leaving children strapped in their car while attending a wine tasting event. So many headlines and stories to distract, entertain, unite, or divide us, on any device, any time, all the time. What's important and what's not? What has an impact and what doesn't? What has become quite obvious is that with all the choices and influences enveloping our existence, we have only one option if we are going to survive and thrive—adapt or die. Sounds harsh, but it's a fact, whether you're an individual, a business, or a community. Did you realize 429 of the original Fortune 500 companies are no longer in business today? Adapt or die. Let's spend a few moments exploring the value of choosing to live our lives in a positive adaptive state.

A mentor of mine once told me to consider the following:

The challenge for us all is discovering how to exercise self-management in the face of change, how to sink into the sweet spot between rational facts and emotional connectivity that propels us forward and allows us to adapt.

He always had words of wisdom to impart. Depending on my state of mind, I either listened with eager anticipation and considered how to apply his words, or I heard him with a numb feeling of confusion and struggled to translate and make use of the advice. Like my mentor, I recognize helping people adapt—evolving core beliefs, values, and cultural norms into a new way of thinking and behaving—is not easy and I don't take it lightly. The topic of adaptation, change, and rebirth is not new. Yet it certainly never seems to get old precisely because it's so difficult to attempt and sustain. No matter the topic or content of adaptation, it requires mindfulness over a period of time, even in the face of life's noise.

Whether it's a small non-profit, a large corporation, a community, or an individual, many are looking for help with this elusive concept of behavioral change—helping people and organizations adjust mind-set in order to change behaviors that lead to improved performance and engagement. There are two fundamental pieces of the puzzle needed to attain and sustain any type of effective change—acceptance and momentum. Nothing matters if you cannot adopt a healthy mind-set of accepting conditions and situational life experiences as a necessary step toward an improved state—no matter how unfair, biased, or irrational things may seem at the time. Further, research supports that any form of self-adaptation, be it direct or causal, begins with a stimulus signaling a change is necessary. Building on that initial stimulus is what creates momentum. Unfortunately, most of us often miss the signals as we push diligently to survive, which usually means maintaining some form of the current state.

To illustrate the importance of acceptance and momentum in order to adapt, one particular session comes to mind. I delivered a strategic planning workshop to a group of roughly 20 executives in the Midwest around the topic of workforce engagement and managing Millennials. Now, this is no start-up we're talking about. It's a company that spent the last hundred or so years building a specific process to hire, train, evaluate, promote, and manage its people a certain way—and that way is now failing. They can no longer attract and retain top Millennial talent. Once Millennials join the organization, not even money can incentivize them to stay if they see an opportunity elsewhere to do something they feel has more purpose. The command and control style of management that once seemed so effective now has Millennials headed for the exit. So what are the options? The organization could maintain the current culture that proved so successful in the past or they could adapt and look for a new way of operating, even if it seems foreign and perhaps even risky.

As expected, everyone in the session was highly credentialed and extremely confident in his/her ability to solve this problem and deliver stellar results. They all had a well-documented paper trail of successes and a combined two centuries worth of experience managing people. As any good consultant does, I asked the first, in a series of $20,000 questions—"What will success look like when we're done?" quickly followed by the $50,000 follow up, "How will we measure it?"

With the wind of bureaucracy at their back and sublime narcissism, several shared their perspectives.

Larry, VP of sales and marketing, began, "We have to change the game, people; enough of playing by the same rules that got us here. Hear me out. We always say we want to stay ahead of the competitive curve. Seriously? Our competitors are spending significant investment dollars on understanding this new workforce. We have to at least get serious about knowing what we're up against before we can talk about what success looks like."

John, the CFO, retorted, "Why does every solution begin with spending more money? We know what our strengths are already. This is a great place to work. Always has been, always will be. As long as we stick to our core strategy and values, we'll be fine. We can't risk changing the very culture that made us successful!"

"That's crap and you know it," said Larry. "The last time we fought this talent war we actually restructured! We took a chance, broke the mold and tried something different. Change is inevitable. No risk, no reward, right?"

"Only in sports and casinos does that thinking have any chance of actually working," said Joe, a quiet, demure individual. To this day I have no idea what Joe's job was.

The Change[5]

Let's take a snapshot of the mind-sets that are driving their behaviors.

- Larry is pushing for 'forward momentum' by using positive disruption as a tactic. "Let's break the mold!"

- John is steadfast in maintaining the status quo. "…stick to the core strategy and values"

- Joe is, well, complacently disengaged

In this example, the stimulus for change was the loss of top talent, low workforce engagement, and high turnover rates all within the Millennial ranks. What they needed to do as a team was align their mind-set around acceptance of this current state without penalty. Doing so would have created a positive space where these very capable executives could have adapted the Millennial management strategy to gain some momentum. Much easier said than done, though. Six months later, things had definitely changed, but the organization continued to struggle with this issue. Why? Of our three main characters, only John the CFO was still in place. The others had… well, changed.

To be clear, I can help individuals see things differently. But if they are not in a state of 'readiness to adapt' then the efforts may result in lackluster results or personal frustration at the lack of forward momentum. This team was experiencing frustration with no plan for how to change and some key mind-set roadblocks. They had very little chance of gaining any type of momentum unless they all recognized and accepted the signals for change.

Now, let's go back to my opening story with Jennifer. Try and 'see yourself' in this situation and determine what your state of mind would be. Remember, you're working hard and generally succeeding, but feel a lot of pressure both at work and at home, and you now have a perception that your manager is not in your corner. To set the full scene, Jennifer was a participant in a standard paired coaching session. It was formulaic on all counts—one manager, one direct report (Jennifer), and a set of organizational themes and goals to address. I had my one-on-one with Jennifer prior to the joint session where her manager would be present. I was able to help Jennifer uncover quite a few things about her personal style that may have been impeding her progress that hinted at the need for adaptation. She was appreciative of the time spent, but was extremely anxious about the joint session.

It began as they all do, very polite in tone with passive aggressive underpinnings interspersed throughout.

David, the manager, spent most of his time trying to get Jennifer to admit she still had 'areas of improvement' to address, but failed to give any specific examples. "You're doing fine, maybe step it up sometimes, but stay the course."

"What does that even mean?" Jennifer replied. "Stay what course? Step it up? I need you to be more clear."

This placation two-step dance went on for what seemed like an eternity, but really was only 25 (very long) minutes. Then a breakthrough surfaced. Jennifer took control. "Look David, I'm juggling a lot of decisions right now in my life. This job is just one of them. You either want me to be successful here or not. I can't necessarily do anything about the decisions that are made behind closed doors. And you know what? It's frustrating to base my sense of value on what others think of me, especially when I am not getting the information I need to change those perceptions. But…what I absolutely can do is change my own perceptions. I'm a great worker, a great mother, and have a great story to tell. If my life were a movie, it would be a drama. The kind with all sorts of plot twists and challenges, but one with an awesome ending that inspires other people. David, you're a character in my movie. You play an important role. I realize that now. But you are not writing the next scene. I am."

David seemed a little shaken at first. But then his acceptance of this version of Jennifer slowly revealed itself. He started displaying active engagement in the conversation. He stopped trying to control the conversation. He became authentically interested and invested in her story. I leveraged this turning point to drive toward a sustainable post-session set of commitments.

Jennifer's lightbulb moment of self-awareness about her own power was her stimulus for change. It affected her words and changed her behavior. Her change became the acceptance and stimulus for David to adjust his thinking. His behavior changed. Momentum was achieved.

As a lifelong student of continuous growth, I believe we all have 'areas for development'. I also believe we can learn from each other—in every situation, every interaction. Thus, I learned something from Jennifer and David that day that has changed the lives of thousands. I began using the myMovie analogy as a learning framework in my leadership sessions to help others manage how they adapt personally and professionally.

Consider this: When confronted with complex decisions, stressful environments, and competing priorities, try viewing life through a cinematic lens and accept that life is simply one long-running movie. The ending is never quite certain and the beginning of each scene is filled with a positive optimism that everything will work out eventually. However, there are ever-changing twists and turns created by the subplots of life, which are created by 7 billion people simultaneously starring in their own movies. At times, it may seem like you're always one scene away from being the hero, executing that amazing rescue, solving the crime, or saving the day, all while never running short of breath, hair always in place, and void of any need to consume or release fluid. The struggle continues, the characters change, and the plot thickens. But understand this. A very well-renowned author is writing the cumulative life lessons displayed in your feature presentation. You.

To the billions of life actors gracing the stage of life, you are absolutely the star of your movie, the producer of your release, and the author of the sequel that opens the first of every month. Every scene has purpose, and as long as you accept where you are, you can adapt. You are most deserving of best actor, best supporting actor, best director, and movie of the year.

So if life is a long-running movie, you need to accept you must aggressively take on the role of being an active writer of the next scene instead of a passive critic that lives to provide scathing reviews. Shape your story, create your arc, develop characters that belong in your story, and edit out any unwelcome footage. From the boiler room to the boardroom exist surreal stories of trials and tribulations, adversity and tragedy. There are unbelievable stories of triumph in times of adversity and accomplishments that will never be captured or recorded. Yet they exist. You exist. And because you do, your story matters. Realize that your plot is interconnected with everyone you come in contact with, be it a casual passing or intentional orchestration. Not only does your story matter, you must subscribe to the notion that you play a character in someone else's life movie every day. Your words, actions, and behaviors can alter the course of the future. Starting today, stop reading your life story and begin writing. Be proud of how the story unfolds because YOU are the author, director, and producer. Most people spend the majority of their lives in reactionary mode questioning the plot twists that derail their plans and dreams. If you don't like the script—change it!

I ran into Jennifer at a business conference a few years later. "I'm so glad to see you!" she said. "I've been meaning to call you, but my movie has been crazy busy—in a good kind of way. I wanted you to know the session with David was really enlightening."

"How so?" I replied.

"I learned more about myself than I ever thought possible. My movie is awesome now and I'm totally writing the script! I usually hate being in those types of sessions and was shocked at how helpful it was."

"Is that a compliment, Jennifer?"

A pause, followed by shifting of weight, and then finally confident eye contact and a smile. "Absolutely."

Reggie Butler

Performance Paradigm LLC

Motivate*Innovate*Inspire

Phone: 813-407-8649

Email: rbutler@performanceparadigm.com

Website: http://performanceparadigm.com

Twitter: http://twitter.com/reginaldbutler

LinkedIn: http://linkedin.com/in/reginaldbutler

Larunce Pipkin

Larunce Pipkin earned his Bachelor Degree in Psychology and his Master's in Education, focusing on Cognition and Problem Solving, from the University of Texas, Austin. Larunce first became an HR trainer and Trainer's trainer. After a variety of jobs, he finally found his passion for helping others. He became a Life Coach and Master Life Coach through Certified Coaches Federation. Then he gained his Practitioner and Master level certifications in NLP, NLP Life Coaching, Hypnotherapy and Time Line Therapy®. His ongoing training and education focuses on Integral Theory through the work of Ken Wilber, and meditation. He has always been on a quest for that which binds us all together from breath to death and beyond. While he is working on finishing his first book and a book with two amazing colleagues (Adam and Richard), he enjoys being a photographer, world traveler, Qigong enthusiast, constant seeker of knowledge, stepfather to Becca, and of course, husband to Mimi.

The Ghost in Your Machine

By Larunce Pipkin

After four books filled with transformation and stories of profound change from several great coaches, what on earth would I write that would keep you reading? More importantly what would be the one thing that you need to hear before you decide to make that leap to become the "you" that you (and maybe your mom) know exists, especially if you haven't had that Aha moment in the previous chapters? I thought I would approach things just a bit differently. I'm not talking about 'out of the box' thinking; I am talking about 'what box?' thinking. Let's take a closer look at how we live, that's right, you and I. We breathe the same air, recycle it, and breathe it out again. No matter who is reading this (you), and no matter where you live, at some point we will both breathe in the air that we have both breathed out. So that is where I will begin.

What wakes you up in the morning? What is the very last thing that you say to yourself that makes you get your lazy butt out of bed? Seriously, stop and think about it. What is the absolute last thing that you say to yourself that, after hitting the snooze button on your phone five times, will get you out of that warm, cozy gilded posturepedic lectus cubicularis? Is it, "Ok, enough, I need to get up now," or "#$%@ I'm going to be late—again," or "Just get up and face it (the world)," or "Awesome, it's time to get up and greet the unlimited possibilities that life has waiting for me"? Chances are, you and I will be saying something similar to the first three responses offered. Anyone who says the latter is a freak! To be fair, I would really like to be that freak one day, wouldn't you? I mean to greet the dawning of every day anticipating the wonders that await you, that would be kind of cool. Now, back to the real world. We live our lives every day doing the things that need to be done, and sometimes not doing the things that need to be done. Then things pile up on us and we get overwhelmed, need a weekend to catch up, a weekend to blow off some steam, a weekend to relax and enjoy family, a weekend alone to recharge. That's a lot of weekends and a lot of things piling up. Through all of this, the frustrations, the unfinished work, the unfinished chores, the undedicated time with family, there you are, left with unformed thoughts and unfinished dreams. Sometimes your dreams may seem so far out of reach, that you feel like they have expired and you are left with a feeling of loss over something you never really had to begin with. It can be a kind of torture. Hell, it is torture. I'm not talking about overcoming great obstacles of a physical nature or surviving a great struggle where you are lying flat at the bottom of a hole determined to lift yourself up and out to a greater life. I am not talking about being the next great inspiring Disney story that will make us all think, "Wow, what a great individual, so strong, so determined, it really motivates me to…..well, to do nothing actually." So we want to stay in our comfy lectus cubicularis until we absolutely have to face it all.

Personally, I do not want to have to overcome such physical struggles or hit rock bottom in order to reinvent myself, but I don't want to be where I am either. There is no story about the person who was happy but desired to be a little more or slightly more happy or wanted to help more people, or to be a better person and make the world a better place. Well, maybe there is, but I am certain it was no blockbuster and as such motivated no one. Where does that leave me, where does that leave you? Your life isn't all that bad: you eat, you sleep, you work, have a few friends, maybe a spouse or partner, you have kids or had kids (but now they are off living their own life), you have a mortgage, a decent car, nice clothes, small children do not scream when they see your face. Life is not bad….but why isn't it great or fantastic? Why aren't you living your dream?

You may have your reasons—people will call them excuses—but they don't know your real struggle, your internal struggle. I'm talking about the struggle with doubts and self-sabotage. They do not understand how convincing you can be at undermining your own dreams and aspirations. You've taught yourself to blame your spouse or your job, but internally you blame you. How on earth are you going to overcome that, especially when your life really isn't all that bad? Let me give that last sentence a little perspective.

How to Boil a Frog—A Live Frog—Without It Caring One Tiny Little Bit.

Get a frog, a pot filled with pond water, and a stove. Put the frog in the pot of pond water and put the pot on the stove. Heat the water ever, ever, ever so slowly so that the frog is not aware of the change in temperature, and is just a happy frog in a pond. After a time, the water will be boiling and the frog is cooked without ever trying to escape its unknown fate.

Scientifically, the story may not be very accurate, but metaphorically we need to take it under advisement. We get used to our life, we get used to our boss, we get used to our job, we get used to not making enough money, we get used to not being really truly happy, we get used to letting go of our dreams, we get used to our lives until we realize that our life is over and we haven't given ourselves the opportunity to live.

Great, so now we are both depressed—what next?

It's ok if you are happy where you are. That is great. There is no reason for you to change; just keep doing what you are doing. However, if there is a nagging inside your head or a sense that there has to be more, or you can see yourself doing something amazing or great, then you owe it to yourself to see what it is and where it will lead you.

The first thing that you must understand above all else is that where you are is perfect for you right now. I want to say that again. Where you are is perfect for you right now. The place to begin is now. Your whole life up to this point has been a process aimed getting you to right now, so do not discount it. Go back, retrace the choices that you made to get you to where you are now—you may see that you could have taken this road or that path, but you didn't. You chose the one that you did for whatever reason and it led you to the "you" that you can now see in the mirror if you dare to look close enough. It doesn't matter that you think you should have reached a specific goal years earlier, or when you had more money or a better haircut. What matters is that you are where you are and that is the best place that you could possibly be. Becoming ok with where you are at is not the same thing as giving up or giving in; it's quite the opposite. Becoming ok with where and who you are gives you the opportunity to move that you to a new level, to a new place, on a new path. There are a variety of ways that you can enrich the understanding of being ok with you and where you are. As a Master Practitioner of NLP (neuro linguistic programming), Hypnosis, and Time Line Therapy®, I would tell you to find an TLT® practitioner in your area and have them help you get rid of any limiting beliefs and decisions that you might have holding you back. But any form of transformative work can help. You might even decide to do it yourself through journaling and shadow work, or you might even try meditation.

Once you can silence the negative reasons that you are where you are, new possibilities will begin to open up to you. How can you possibly see new possibilities when you are caught up in all the reasons why you cannot do something or be someone else? So, you may be asking yourself, "How do I silence those negative thoughts and reasons?" It is both very simple and incredibly hard at the same time. Trust!

"That's it, trust? I've been reading this for 10 minutes and all I get is 'Trust'?"

Yes, for now that's the beginning, you have to trust you. You have to trust that you are the person that is in charge of your life and in charge of your outcome. In NLP, you learn that your unconscious is there to help you create the life that you desire, but you have to feed it the proper food. You already trust it to keep you alive when you shut your eyelids at night, to keep your blood pumping and your lungs moving air about. You trust it to store your memories and repress bad things that happen to you, to maintain all of your instincts and generate your habits, so why not trust it to help you get what you want by feeding it the proper food. Wait a minute, you know where I am going with this, don't you? You are absolutely right, the proper food is the thoughts that you feed to your unconscious. Your unconscious does not process negatives directly. You cannot focus on what you do not want in order to get what you want. I totally have to say this with you again out loud.

Repeat with me, "You cannot focus on what you do not want in order to get what you want!"

For example, if you believe that you need to lose weight, do you say, "I do not want to be fat," or do you say, "I want to be healthy?" Those are two very distinct ways of looking at losing weight. One focuses on what the person doesn't want and the other focuses on what the person wants. In the first case, the unconscious will hear, "I want to be Fat" and in the second the unconscious will hear, "I want to be Healthy." The first case will not get you the outcome that you desire, the second will.

So what do you do? Step one is to remove all negatives from your thoughts and your words—thank you, the end. You may think that it cannot be that simple. But it is. Is it hard work? Yes. Does it take practice? Yes. Does it take consistency? Yes. Will you see results?

Yes, unequivocally! Your new mantra could be "I CAN," rather than all the reasons why you cannot. Remember, you got exactly where you are by doing exactly what you have been doing; now it's time to do something different. Too harsh, I do not think so. There is that nagging specter somewhere deep inside you that says that you are more than the mirror and more than what the world sees. There is that sense that given the opportunity, you can do something great for the world (even if the world is just you and your family). This is your opportunity. This is the part that makes me cry for all the possibilities that are inside of you that you have given up on and do not believe deserve to see the light of day.

Once you silence those reasons and are ready to move forward, you will need to learn step two. Learn to listen. Listening is the one thing that we think we can all do very well, but it is actually quite hard. How do you listen? What do you listen to? What are you listening for? When someone is speaking to you, are you busy thinking of what you are going to say next? Maybe you are judging what they are saying while you are listening. Maybe you are thinking of what you need to do tomorrow while they are talking, while waiting for your turn to be 'listened' to. Listening is hard! You can begin to listen with intention. Intention has two main meanings. One meaning is a thing intended; an aim or plan. The second is the healing process of a wound. It is time to create that intention and mend your listening process. Listening also requires you to lessen your own thoughts; it requires that you create bits of silence in your mind where there is no judgement so that your unconscious can digest what is being said. The silence only exists in-between your thoughts. Contrary to popular belief, we (you and I) cannot multitask. The brain is very linear and can only focus on one thing at a time. Being powerful, it can do this so incredibly fast that it seems like multiple things are happening at once, but what it is doing is just starting one thing, stopping it; starting another, stopping it;

and starting another. This is what I am talking about, thoughts [space] thoughts [space] thoughts [space] thoughts [space] thoughts.

Most times, the space between the thoughts is squeezed so tightly it seems that there is no space at all. Silence helps us to widen that space to allow our unconscious to do the things that it needs to do to get us to where we really want to go. One way to mend your listening through silence is with meditation. Meditation will help you effectively widen that space between your thoughts, which can have a profound effect on the quality and direction of your life.

A quick, very quick intro to meditation: combining what you learned from step one and step two.

Find a quiet place, a place where you can be alone and undisturbed for 20-30 minutes. Ask yourself what it is that you want, then just sit in silence and listen. Listen without conjuring up the reasons and without the excuses. Just listen to the silence and wait for the answer of what you want to come to you, then listen to the silence again. It doesn't matter what comes to you, just let it come to you and then just let it go and sit in the silence. Do this every day, twice a day. Sit in the silence between your thoughts and when you have a thought, dismiss it and go back to that silence between your thoughts. I like to call it the gap (from Deepak Chopra), it reminds me of a few trips I took to Europe when I would ride the tube (underground rail). As you were boarding every train, there was a sign that looked like all of the station signs or an audible recording that said, "Mind the Gap" My first time pretending to be a Londoner, I had no idea what it meant. I was surprised to learn that it was a warning to be aware of the gap between the rail platform and the train car as you stepped to board the train. It has taken on a new meaning for me. You have to "mind the gap" in order to get from where you are (the platform where you are stuck) to where you want to go (your dreams and aspirations). Go ahead use it to help you back to the silence, I don't mind.

It doesn't matter if that silence (gap) only lasts for a second or two, just keep going back to it, over and over until that 20-30 minutes is done. Then do it the next day and the next. It may be difficult at first but it will get easier and easier as you consistently practice each day. Every athlete has a routine that he goes back to in order to improve his game; let this be your routine. Every CEO has a practice that is her time and serves to get her realigned with her vision; let this be your vision. Every religion has its ritual that serves to bring both the leaders and the followers back to their foundation; let this be your religion.

Let there be no mistake—this is work. This is your sport, this is your organization, this is your religion and it requires dedication and practice. You do not become a concert pianist in a month; it takes at least five years of intentional solid daily practice. My martial arts instructor used to say that a decent roundhouse kick could not be seen or improved upon until after 10,000 kicks. Buddha lived as an ascetic for 6 years until he finally sat under the Bodhi Tree, and some texts say that he did that for 7 weeks before gaining enlightenment. If you are going to model excellence as we do in NLP, I would say that 7 weeks seems like an especially reasonable amount of time to spend creating the path that you know will give you your dreams.

What you are engaged in is vertical cognitive growth; some people just call it meditation. What it does for you over repeated sessions is awaken that Ghost in Your Machine. That dream, that realization of who you really truly are supposed to be. But it does more than just wake that Ghost of infinite possibilities that is you—it fosters it, it grooms it, it makes it undeniable, and when that happens you will have no choice but to lift yourself out of that comfortable pot of boiling water, out of that lectus cubicularis of slumber and create the life that you were destined to create. The Ghost in Your Machine is more than just a nod to the beginnings of the mind-body struggle; it is the acknowledgment from me that I see all the universe and all of the infinite possibilities alive in you.

To contact Larunce:

Website: www.NLP-4Success.com

Twitter: @LarunceNLP

Facebook: facebook.com/NLP4Success

Or ask him any questions at Larunce@NLP-4Success.com

Lauren Perotti

Lauren Perotti is a Life Purpose and Prosperity Speaker, Author, and Coach. She delivered her first keynote talk as the valedictorian of her 1968 graduating class—Catholic kindergarten! With sparkle and humor, Lauren has delivered messages of leadership, inspiration, and what it takes to triumph in the ABCs of life on many stages and pages in the years since. She is co-author of several books, and is working on her book *Ignite the Fire of Your Purpose, Passion, and Power: 7 Spiritual Pillars to Light Your Path to Pure Prosperity.*

Blending 30 years of expertise in business, psychology, and the arts, Lauren coaches spiritual-seeking professionals whose success rings hollow and who feel disconnected from their fire inside to create a prosperous life they love in all realms. Her programs are built on the proven art and science of DreamBuilding together with spirituality and creative arts practices.

Lauren is your advocate for living your passion. She lives her own by traveling with her sweetheart, singing and skipping along her Yellow Brick Road, and leading others she meets along the way to discover that on their way to Oz, what they seek is already within them.

Reach For the Light

Discover Your Purpose, Live Your Passion

By Lauren Perotti

Reach for the light, you might touch the sky
Stand on the mountaintop, and see yourself flying
Reach for the light, to capture a star
Come out of the darkness, and find out who you are

~ Steve Winwood

Have you been tremendously distressed by your life's challenges? Whether you are a seasoned executive whose success rings hollow, a busy professional stuck on the treadmill of never-ending responsibilities, or *anyone* who feels disconnected from your *FIRE* inside, you may feel in the dark, or even as if part of you is dying.

When you're not able to fully express your spirit, gifts, character traits, and honed skills that make you unique, you may start to feel dull. If you're shut down for a long enough time, you may experience what some call a dark night of the soul.

Yet you are like a diamond—unique, multifaceted, and designed to receive and reflect light. Just as it takes tremendous heat and pressure deep in the earth to transform carbon into a brilliant natural diamond, sometimes your highest human potential comes through dark times and fiery trials. What if your stress and darkness could be a catalyst to ignite your resurrecting power within?

The Talmud, a sacred ancient text of Rabbinic Judaism, says that "Every blade of grass has its angel that bends over it and whispers,

'Grow, grow.'" Just imagine what that blade of grass must do in order to keep growing; it presses through soil, sometimes even cement, to seek the light. What a seemingly hard task! Sometimes your human quest to live more of who you really are and do more of what you love can feel that hard. But you are also designed to reach for the light and to desire more expression of that which is in your very DNA.

Your DNA is shaped in a spiral, and you live in a spiral universe that is ever expanding—is this a coincidence? We are each a spark of the universe, which is our extended body; this is not merely a profession of faith, but a law of physics.

If every element in creation has a unique purpose, so too do you and I. The more you not only understand your life purpose but live in alignment with it, the more everything and everyone around you will empower your ability to manifest your greatest dreams.

My Resurrection

When I was a very young girl, I was afraid of the dark. Many children have this fear, but mine was not really as much about scary monsters or things of that nature. My fear of darkness came from feeling like I was on my own and disconnected from the light of my spirit. It felt as if I were missing part of me that left a dark hole inside, causing me to wonder, "Why am I here?"

I came to understand why I felt this separation much later in life, but even back then, this feeling stirred my lifelong quest to look for the light that could fill that black hole and show me the way.

What is this light I am talking about? For me, it comes from awareness and wisdom, from deep connection to others and ultimately, from knowing, expressing, and living my life purpose.

As a young woman, my self-identity unconsciously came from other people, places, and things. By that time, I was seemingly thriving as a senior manager in an international accounting firm, living in a beautiful Newport Beach townhouse, and looking successful. I had climbed that corporate ladder quickly and was primed for a promotion to partner in the firm.

I had already gone through the crumbling of my marriage, which made me painfully aware again of that black hole. Since then, I had spent several years on my own personal development quest; I engaged in psychotherapy, spiritual and personality assessment systems such as the Myers'-Briggs, Enneagram, Numerology, Astrology, and more. You can easily find assessment tests for these systems online and they are insightful. I uncovered and healed some childhood wounds, was working on others, and had begun to get a sense of who I really was and the life I'd love to be living.

With that awakening came my increasing discontent with the deadline-driven demands of that career, which kept me focused on meeting and exceeding others' needs and expectations at my own expense. This environment mirrored that of my childhood family, in which my role was to create order out of chaos. My life was out of balance, and I wasn't engaging in my passions—singing, the arts, and spirituality. Although there were ways I felt satisfied in this career, there were too many of my talents that were being suppressed. I thirsted for something more meaningful, but I felt STUCK. I kept on running that rat race because I saw no viable way out.

So what happened? My body failed—and bailed me out. I started feeling run down, but convinced myself I was working too hard and just needed a break. Pretty quickly, my symptoms grew—fevers and night sweats, lightheadedness to the point of nearly fainting, and unexplained bruises. Clearly something was wrong, but I still kept on running.

While at an out-of-town conference, I happened to brush my leg against a table, which immediately brought up a huge, hard black bruise. Now I was scared. When I got back to my hotel room that evening, I stared in the mirror at my pale face and bruised body and couldn't ignore this any longer. I took myself to the emergency room, where I was shockingly diagnosed with Acute Leukemia. My dis-ease had seeped down to the core of my bones, into the marrow, and was surging through my blood.

So began another transforming journey. I spent the better part of that year in hospitalized isolation, connected 24/7 to a surgically implanted catheter in my chest that was being infused with large volumes of nuclear level chemo, blood, antibiotics, and more that I needed to sustain my life. I could not leave the room or detach from the IV pole. Yet, paradoxically, after the initial shock of the diagnosis, instead of feeling stuck, I was freer and more joyful than I had ever been.

How could this be true? Wouldn't such a physical and existential trial be like a wild rollercoaster ride through pain and fear, to hope, to doubt and back up again for any human being, especially over such a long time period? Can I live or will I die? At times, my body felt nearly as ravaged by my harrowing treatment as that of Jesus Christ at his crucifixion, with whom I identified during this journey that began near Eastertime. Just as he shed his blood for our salvation, my own blood was being purified for MY redemption—and a new life. Therein lied my hope. Other factors helped me reach for the light amid dark moments.

First, I was connected to a community and surrounded by waves of love. It touched me, then expanded outward in ever-widening circles, like those created when you toss a pebble into a pond. It came from family, friends, neighbors, owners of businesses I patronized, my fabulous team of doctors, Jesus and the Angels, and even business colleagues from the very firm I had been trying so hard to leave! The more I absorbed the love, the more my life force energy was able to vibrate at a higher level, which elicits healing and joy.

Second, being isolated gave me the opportunity to learn how to become acutely present in the here and now, which is where the kingdom of heaven truly resides.

Third, I transformed what could have been a sterile hospital room into a studio for life-giving creativity—music, singing, and art. I sang from the core of my being, and I discovered my truth—that I am a creative, passionate light worker who also happens to have savvy business and finance acumen. I can and do work with both of these seemingly different aspects of my whole Self.

Finally, deep down, I knew that my very survival depended on loving myself enough to fully forgive and release past hurts, claim my life purpose, and live my passion. This resolve, and the angels leaning over me, activated the resurrecting power in me.

Transformational Wisdom

Since then, I discovered many more powerful sources of transformation and self-discovery. In addition to the spirituality and personality systems mentioned above, I've studied and work with the natural elements, the chakras, angelic guidance, creative arts processes, and symbolic and archetypal imagery as tools to keep growing. Here's a summary of wisdom from these sources, along with suggestions to begin working with them.

The Natural Elements

Elements of nature play a significant role in generating and activating the flow of energy. Intentionally engaging with them maximizes your ability to manifest and live your life purpose.

Earth. Earth is the foundation upon which you build the life you desire, grounding you in the here and now. Earth is one element of presence, your purpose, and the first chakra. When your spirit resides in your body, and your body is grounded to the earth, you experience a fuller sense and feeling of "who I am." This fuller sense of presence enhances your ability to know what you're here to do.

Action: Walk barefoot in the park and sense earth's gravitational energy, see the beauty of a colorful garden, smell the fragrant flowers and taste their nectar, hear the birds singing in the trees.

Water. Water is fluid and facilitates the natural flow and unfolding of your path. Water is the element of creativity and of the second chakra. It represents your ability to be emotionally expressive and playful. Water is about curiosity, and if you're willing to dive down a little below the surface to see what's there, you may be surprised at what you'll find.

Action: Connect with water. Take a walk near a beach, lake, pond, or stream. Observe and even touch its flow. Luxuriate in a hot bath.

Fire. Fire burns away illusions, ignites your passion, and lights the way. Fire is the element of your personal power and the third chakra. It is active; it moves and can spread quickly when unleashed.

Action: Do a "Breath of Fire" exercise for a minute. This involves pumping your naval area in and out while you breathe rapidly through your nostrils. To make this even more powerful, visualize a fiery, expanding ball of energy in your belly as you do it.

Air. Air provides freshness and clarity. Air is the element of the heart chakra, which also fuels the fire of passion. Like fire, air is also about movement. In addition to feeling refreshing, a nice breeze or wind can signify change and rebirth.

Action: Find a song that expresses a message with which you resonate—particularly one that may speak to an aspect of your truth that you have been holding in. Play the song and sing along with it.

The Chakras

All forms of matter vibrate at various energetic frequencies. You and I are no exception. The chakras are centers of energy in your subtle body (i.e., they are not physical, but are near specific physical body parts); they are portals for receiving the light energy from this spiraling, ever-expanding universe.

They also help your vital life force flow through your entire being. Activating your chakras is one of the most potent sources for feeling fully alive. The elements of earth, water, fire, and air influence the first four chakras; the upper chakras are associated with the cosmic elements of ether, light, and spirit.

Here is a simple description of each:

> **Chakra 1.** Your root chakra is the very foundation of your core survival (health and prosperity), trust, and family (tribe) association. Its color of light is red.
>
> **Chakra 2.** Your sacral chakra relates to pleasure, play, creativity, feelings and sensations, and being in the moment. Its color of light is orange.
>
> **Chakra 3.** The solar plexus chakra activates self-esteem, personal power. and the will to move forward and get things done. Its color of light is yellow.
>
> **Chakra 4.** Your heart chakra is associated with love, passion, and healing. Its color of light is green.

Chakra 5. Your throat chakra activates self-expression, your ability to speak your truth, and manifest your goals and desires. Its color of light is blue.

Chakra 6. This is the brow chakra, otherwise known as the "third eye." It is essential for activating perception, intuition, imagination, and "seeing" possibilities. Its color of light is indigo.

Chakra 7. Your crown chakra is the primary portal for connecting to your own spiritual nature and the Divine, God, or whatever you may personally call the spirit that is greater than you are. Its color of light is violet.

Action: Reflect on which chakras you want to empower. Place yourself in a meditative space and ground yourself. Visualize the color that relates to the chakra you're working on swirling around the area it resides within your body.

The Angels

You don't have to subscribe to a religion to believe in the existence of angels. The term "angel" is really more our earthly human word for these multidimensional beings of light that serve as protectors, guardians, divine messengers, and so much more.

Here are some ways particular angels can help you reach your highest potential:

Archangel Michael. Known as the Great Prince, this powerful Protector guards both your physical body and spiritual destiny. He is immensely helpful for transforming negative energy within and without into peace, love, and beauty.

Archangel Jophiel. When you want to discover more of your light within and the vision of what you desire, this angel of Creative Power, inspiration, and beauty can guide you.

Angel Sandalphon. If you are grappling with any fears or blocks about expressing your gifts and talents, this angel helps you name, claim, and aim your personal power.

Archangel Hadraniel. This heart angel helps awaken your memory of eternal love, which is ultimately all that your soul needs. This can help you cultivate more love in your relationships.

Archangel Raphael. If you want to establish wholeness and balance, ask this Divine Healer to shower you with powerful healing and love energy.

Archangel Gabriel. This Messenger angel announces your Divine mission, and inspires and motivates your artistic communications. He helps break through your procrastination so you can move forward to fulfill your purpose.

Angel Ongkanon. As you continue to enhance your communication with family members and other loved ones, this angel can greatly assist you to gain the higher meaning when strong feelings arise and express them with clarity.

Angel Paschar. When you desire to create a clear vision for what's next, this angel helps you enhance your intuition and perception.

Archangel Zadkiel. This angel of Prayer guards the powers of invocation.

Action: Talk to any angel about what you want just as you would a human friend either in meditation, out loud, or in writing. Look for signs of divine communication from them, particularly through the universal language of numbers and music.

The Creative Arts and Symbolic Imagery

Creative expression is about making time to play or create something—just for the fun of doing it. It could be a culinary dish, a dance, a poem, singing a song, drawing freely—whatever it is that you love to do, without an end goal in mind!

When you immerse in a creative process with any of the artistic disciplines, such as visual art, language arts, music, dance, drama, and ritual arts, it literally helps you become present because you use your senses. You also automatically tap into your imagination, which is how you can bring the unconscious into tangible form, and into the light of awareness. The same holds true when you allow yourself to play and have fun.

This is not unique to current times. The practice of creative expression goes back a long way, to the very beginning of human life when primitive man etched images in his cave dwelling where he surely also danced and sang his story!

Engaging in the arts and recreation is life giving. The creative process mirrors the natural cycle of creation that generates all life forms. It begins in the formless pool of pure potentiality (water), out of which a thought or idea arises (air), and then becomes form through a material grounding process (earth). Eventually, that which you create breaks down—or you let it go—and it becomes formless again, starting the cycle anew.

Symbolic imagery and archetypes are yet another dimension of the creative realm. Jung was the first psychologist of his time to understand the transforming power of imagery in the path to Self-actualization through the symbolic process.

Tarot or oracle cards are a powerful tool for working with symbolic imagery and archetypes. While there are some who use this as a fortune-telling vehicle, I have found it to be more potent when used as a map to explore the current themes surrounding you and your life.

Action: Visualize your dream life. Set aside focused time away from all your to-dos and ask yourself "What would I love, if time or money were not an issue"? Play inspiring music, meditate on this question, and picture yourself living your dream life, without wondering HOW it will happen. Then write down whatever comes to your mind, no matter how impossible it may appear. Finally, create a vision board representing this life you just envisioned using images and words from magazines or other sources that inspire you.

If you confidently take any of these suggested action steps in the direction of your dream, you will begin to experience more joy, freedom and harmony—and THAT is Pure Prosperity beyond any success you've ever known.

To contact Lauren:

Website: www.LaurenPerotti.com

Facebook: www.facebook.com/laurenperotticoaching

LinkedIn: www.LinkedIn.com/pub/lauren-perotti/5/1a9/884/

Email: lauren@laurenperotti.com

Sandi Cohen, BS and Ed Cohen, RPh

"You are where your thoughts are.

Make sure your thoughts are where you want to be."

Sandi and Ed are best-selling contributing authors, and international speakers with a huge national and international following. They live by the mantra, No One Left Behind.

Sandi and Ed reside in a prestigious Nevada community, Lake Las Vegas, and Ed is an avid golfer.

Sandi and Ed are fiercely committed to guiding others to achieve financial and spiritual success and achieve POM (Peace of Mind) so they too can Live Life as It Should Be!

They have been on a path of mentorship for over two decades when they realized they could help others through what they learned from their experiences.

Sandi and Ed have led by example to hundreds of thousands, and personally mentored 48 families to achieve million-dollar status.

Sandi and Ed are Co-Founders and Board members of the ANMP (Association of Network Marketing Professionals), and featured in an Amazon best-seller, and several other publications. Sandi was awarded the prestigious honor of being Woman of the Year by the peers in her current company.

The Change[5]

Sandi and Ed are both graduates of Temple University in Philadelphia, PA, culminating in a degree in Pharmacy for Ed and a BS in Education for Sandi.

Ed served six years in the Army Reserve.

Sliding Doors

By Sandi Cohen, BS and Ed Cohen, RPh

Imagine being in your early 50's, $450,000 in debt, and in a downward spiral that does not seem to end. When you think things can't possibly get worse, they usually do.

In the first sentence in Dr. Scott Peck's book *The Road Less Traveled,* he states, "Life is difficult." As soon as we learn to accept this, the road to stability and a joyful life can begin.

We all have had conflicts in the past, causing us huge amounts of pain. The pain becomes as intense as we allow it to become. When that pain is gone and we have dealt with it, the reality is that we will have to deal with pain again. No one we know can navigate their way through life without some difficulties. This applies to the average person as well as the millionaire or billionaire.

Pain and suffering play no favorites and we all have to deal with challenge eventually. It is how you deal with your challenge that determines the solution.

It's easy to say, "Woe is me," and play the victim. Everything and everybody is against me. There is no hope, no future. How do we turn that around? How do we choose the correct turn at the fork in the road of life? Life is about choices. We have the option to make those choices, to choose the direction in which we are headed.

We have a friend who we lovingly call Pauline. That's not her real name. If you're are old enough, and I doubt too many of you are, it refers to a character in a serial movie in the early twentieth century called *The Perils of Pauline*. Pauline always had to get out of a perilous situation in each episode. It was like she attracted trouble. Catastrophes happened to Pauline, but she always seemed to escape. Our friend is like Pauline, always having something come up that would interfere with life. Do you know anyone like Pauline? Someone you cannot count on to be where he or she has to be and adhere to his or her commitments.

The cat got sick. The dog died. I broke a leg. My cousin passed away. These are all valid excuses; however, some people attract these events more than others, and that is Pauline. The one thing we know in advance is that Pauline will always have some negative event come up in the future.

What does this have to do with our story? First of all, we were Pauline once. At some point in our life, everything was going wrong. Life was a series of Murphy's Law at its finest. If something could go wrong, it usually did. And so we began our transition from a feeling of hopelessness to where we are today.

We met in 1956 at a neighborhood center dance on a Friday night. It was love at first sight. I was blinded by the aura Sandi gave off, and then realized it was the reflection of light from her dental braces. But yes, I was attracted to Sandi, but she was attracted to my friend. Our first date was a Fraternity rush party. We dated on and off for five years and married in 1961.

I opened my first pharmacy in 1961 after my discharge from the army. It was the first of several partnerships and lasted all of nine months. I was working 80 hours a week for a draw of forty dollars a week, which was not enough to cover our monthly expenses. Sandi took a job as a cosmetic sale person doing demonstrations in beauty salons on Saturdays as she finished her college career at Temple University to obtain a BS in elementary education. I, meanwhile, purchased our next pharmacy in 1967 in the West Philadelphia area when the owner died. Three years later, another pharmacy owner a city block away passed away and I was approached to buy that business also. This led to a total of five pharmacies in six years. Sandi started a medical supply company in the front of one of the pharmacies, building it to a multimillion dollar company in three years with a specialty in pediatrics, making a positive impact on families with children with special needs.

We thought we were set for life. We had a 10,000 square foot home in suburban Philadelphia, a Rolls Royce, a stretch limo, an English houseman, a cook from Grand Cayman, and a condo in Florida. Life was good and we never thought it would ever change. But, change happens and sometimes it's a positive change and sometimes it goes the other way.

In 1984, Medicare, which was our largest account receivable, changed its guidelines. Our carrier, Pennsylvania Blue Cross, needed six months to change their software to comply with the new guidelines.

We had six months of having to make payroll every Friday, despite the fact that there was no cash flow. Imagine having a million dollars in receivables, a half a million in inventory, 36 employees that wanted to get paid every Friday, and no cash flow. We leveraged as much as we could, but it became evident that it was time for us to sell or file for bankruptcy. Bankruptcy was not an option because we did not want our 36 employees to suffer, so we looked for a buyer.

In March of 1986, we entered into an agreement of sale with a group of accountants and attorneys. We were to stay on as Vice-Presidents and hold 10% of the new company. This is when life for us really changed. We hadn't worked for anyone else in over 20 years, so this was new to us. We had trepidations about the contract initially and our concerns turned out to be fact. Nine months after they took over, they were requiring a loan from a bank and when we refused to subordinate what they owed us to a million and a half dollar loan, we were terminated. We filed a multimillion dollar lawsuit against our former employers in January of 1987.

The litigation went on for eight years in the Philadelphia court system. In the meantime, we moved to Phoenix in 1993 to try to start over. We were now dead broke and $450,000.00 in debt. We moved into a small townhouse in Fountain Hills, Arizona, sharing a 10-year-old car with no air conditioning. Sandi's mother, living in Florida, became very ill and we moved her to Arizona to live with us for five years with 24 hour a day care, being diapered, suctioned, tube fed, and on oxygen before she passed away. We had to scrape together money to help pay for her care and eventually had to pawn some of Sandi's jewelry and after we couldn't make the payments, we lost them to the pawnshop.

We had no one to turn to, but quitting was never an option. I had taken the State Board Pharmacy exams in both Arizona and Nevada, so I obtained a job with a supermarket chain. Our debt structure was such that some months we couldn't pay the electric bill and the phone bill. The electric company could not shut off the electricity because of the life support issue, so sometimes we were without phones. Still, we didn't quit. We knew there had to be an answer. We knew "Life is difficult," but this was a little much. We would go to sleep crying and wake up crying, saying, "When will the pain end?" Was there hope? We were only looking for what we called POM (Peace of Mind) and that means being able to pay the bills at the end of the month, not having too much month left at the end of the money.

This is when Sandi became aware of Esther and Jerry Hicks and the teachings of Abraham. This was a dramatic turn-around in our way of thinking and had an enormous effect on our future.

When we moved to Arizona, Sandi had lunch with a woman she was introduced to by a friend. They discussed what the options were to get us out of our situation. Getting a teacher's position was out of the question because in Arizona they only paid teachers about $25,000.00 a year and we needed more than that a month to satisfy our debt.

The woman asked, "Have you ever heard of network marketing?" Sandi explained that I was adamantly opposed to Network Marketing since five years earlier, Sandi convinced me to purchase $8,000 worth of water filters from NSA that we couldn't sell and finally gave to Goodwill Industries. I made Sandi promise never to do Network Marketing again. But the universe in all its greatness had sent this woman to us for a reason.

That lunch meeting was the start of our career in Network Marketing.

The first three years in the Network Marketing business model were difficult but a huge learning experience. We were involved in phone card deals, diet patches, thigh cream etc. Our phone bills were more than any compensation we ever received.

But finally, in 1995, after working in nine different companies, we found a company we stayed with for seven years. The biggest nightmare was they started changing the compensation plan and not to the advantage of the Independent Business Owners.

In 1995, our litigation was finally going to trial. We had selected a jury on a Friday afternoon, but the judge had other ideas. He understood that there were complexities in the case that could take weeks or months before a juror could understand. He got the defendants in a room and forced them to settle. It was such a small settlement that the only winners were the attorneys.

The Change[5]

Life is about choices. At some point, in the course of time, a decision has to be made. The door we choose determines our future. We saw a movie several years ago called *Sliding Doors*. It was based on the premise that even the slightest move in one direction could affect the rest of your life, or not.

Have you ever attended an event that you were coerced to go to and met someone who became a life-long friend, and a part of your life? Had you not gone to that event, you would have never met that person and experienced the joy of that relationship? The movie showed what would happen in either case. We believe that nothing happens by chance. It is pre-determined in the universe that you were to meet that special person, so you are led to the right sliding door. Think about it. If you didn't make the decisions you made, would your life be different today? Would you want it to be different?

In the past, we had many decisions that had to be made. Did we make the right ones? Only time and our legacy will tell.

Each was another sliding door.

The first *Sliding Door* we chose was to attend that Friday night dance at the neighborhood center in northeast Philadelphia. We met, and now have been married for over 53 years. If either one of us stayed home that night, this story would not have been written.

The next *Sliding Door* was to make the decision to get married and start a family. We have been blessed with two sons and five grandchildren.

After being bought out by our partner in our first pharmacy, I worked for various pharmacies for five years, but longed to have my own business again.

In passing, I was told by a fellow employee about his friend who passed away and the family wanting to sell their business. Had he not mentioned it, I would never have known about the opportunity.

Another *Sliding Door* because that purchase was our first step in achieving the lifestyle we dreamed of.

The pharmacy was in a less than ideal neighborhood that we used to avoid even driving through. The choice was made and we owned that pharmacy for 25 years. We became very active in the community and established a Medical Center that served the area and later was acquired by Philadelphia College of Osteopathic Medicine.

After acquiring four more pharmacies over the next four years, there came a time that we became overextended. We had a large employee theft problem at one of the pharmacies and we were on the verge of filing bankruptcy. Our attorneys and accountants advised us that the 10,000 square foot house should be sold. We selfishly did not want to do that because we had emotional ties to the home. Another choice had to be made. It was another *Sliding Door*.

In 1978, a customer came into one of our pharmacies and asked Sandi about a particular item she needed for her mother. Sandi inquired and found out how simple it was to supply the item and get insurance to pay for it. That was the start of our multimillion dollar a year medical supply company. It was a decision that saved our home and gave us the lifestyle described earlier. Another *Sliding Door*... that customer had choices, but she came to us.

Sandi's decision to finally call the woman after being in Arizona for 3 months became another *Sliding Door*. Had she not called, Network Marketing would never have been an option.

Time after time, these *Sliding Doors* played a huge part in our future.

The Change[5]

Have you ever looked back and wondered?

What would have happened if you just turned left one day instead of right? We have made those decisions and have no regrets about what our life was, is, and will be. We can never know where the other doors would have taken us, we can only guess. No regrets. Our life took a dramatic change. Change is sometimes difficult. Some people can adjust to change and others find it impossible. When change is positive, it is easy to adjust, but when change becomes negative, it can affect your entire physical and mental well-being.

If you have ever read the book *Who Moved My Cheese?* You know that change affects different people in different ways. When the cheese was moved and eventually disappeared, Sniff went looking for the cheese through the maze as if his life depended on it. The others just sat back and hoped that the cheese would somehow reappear.

In October 2002, we received a call from a man we didn't know, who told us there was a startup company he wanted us to take a look at.

We asked what was the name, the product, who were the owners, and what was the compensation plan? To all these he answered "can't tell you, can't tell you." He said we'd have to sign a non-disclosure and fly to Utah to take a look. We were already with a company for seven years and not looking to change, especially with the failure rate of startups. It was at that point a *Sliding Door* appeared. Do we go to Utah or stay at home?

We apparently made the right choice, because that trip to Utah was our cheese. We asked the man, "What do we need to do to be successful quickly?" We knew our check with our present company would be in jeopardy. His advice was, "Work like your life depends on it for six months." That's what we did and the results were beyond anything we had imagined. If we stayed home and didn't make that trip to Utah, who knows what our life would be like today.

We have been responsible for helping 48 families earn over a million dollars each in the last 12 years. And conversely, our team has helped us become multimillion dollar earners. All due to being of service to others.

It's amazing that through all the stress and pain, we always had hope and faith that we would find our cheese again. Stress on a relationship due to the lack of money can be a disaster. Yet, over 54 years we have survived knowing in our hearts that God didn't want us to suffer. We just wanted our life back and the Peace of Mind that comes with financial freedom.

We had to change our mind-set from retail businesses with employees, huge inventories, accounts receivable, accounts payable, and huge payrolls each week to working from home with none of the above.

The number one barrier stopping people cold is the inability to make decisions.

We changed the area of the country we lived in so we could enjoy over 300 days of sunshine rather than the cold, snow, and ice of the Northeast.

When change appears, you must be ready to make a decision.

The difference between successful people and those that struggle is that successful people make decisions quickly. Successful people weigh the pros and cons and make a decision quickly without "hemming" and "hawing."

The Change[5]

The past had been difficult. We had it all and lost it. We've got it back and we intend to keep it. Success comes after years of hard work, not by winning the lottery.

We now live in a beautiful community in Henderson called Lake Las Vegas. I play golf three times a week as well as working our business.

Our income now allows us to do what we want, when we want, as well as others to do the same. It has also allowed us to help the charities of our choice.

If you're stuck and in need of change this is our Blueprint that can lead you to success.

>   *P*atience. It's not a race.

>   *P*ersistent. Never give up.

>   *P*ersonal Growth. It's who you become in the process.

>   *P*ositive. You are where your thoughts are. Make sure your thoughts are where you want to be.

>   *P*assion. Belief in what you are doing

>   *P*urpose. What will make your heart sing when you wake up?

>   *P*eople. Helping people be all they can be.

Life is about choices.

It's never too late to Live Life as It Should Be!

"Look to this Day". Yesterday is already a dream. Tomorrow is only a vision. But, each day well lived makes every yesterday a dream of happiness and every tomorrow a vision of Hope." —Sanskrit Proverb

---

To contact Sandi & Ed:

Website: www.SandiandEd.com

Email: Sandi@SandiandEd.com

Facebook: www.Facebook.com/Sandi.Cohen2

Facebook: www.Facebook.com/Forever50movement

Telephone: (702) 381-3799

Jacqueline Haessly

Jacqueline Haessly, PhD, serves as president of *Peacemaking Associates,* where she works as a peace education specialist. Jackie joyfully educates and empowers people of all ages to value, imagine, and act to preserve a culture of peace in all the dimensions of their lives—the family, the community, and the world. Her *Peacemaking* workshops and keynote addresses have been presented to audiences in both North and South America, as well as in Africa and Europe.

Jackie's published works include *Peacemaking: Family Activities for Justice and Peace*, Volume One and Two and *Weaving a Culture of Peace*. Her work is also included as chapters in education and business publications, including *When the Canary Stops Singing: Women's Perspectives on Transforming Business*, *Working Together: Producing Synergy by Honoring Diversity*, and *Tourism, Progress, and Peace,* among others. Her more recent work has focused on *Franciscan Values and the Art and Act of Peacemaking*.

Jackie received her undergraduate and graduate degrees from the University of Wisconsin-Milwaukee and Cardinal Stritch University. She earned her PhD in Interdisciplinary Studies with an emphasis on Spirituality, Peace, and Transformational Leadership from The Union Institute and University in 2001.

Jackie enjoys sailing, swimming, knitting, mysteries, and grand parenting.

Transformation for a Culture of Peace

Jacqueline Haessly, PhD

The twenty-first century opened with a challenge from the United Nations General Assembly, one issued at the behest of the Nobel Peace Prize Laureates who urged all peoples and their government officials to work together at the local, regional, national, and international levels to promote a culture of peace and nonviolence for all of the children of the world. Rather than peace, we have witnessed throughout the early years of this century horrific acts of terrorism, genocide, and ceaseless wars. Receiving less media attention, and therefore less known to most of us, are the effective nonviolent efforts for peace taking place throughout the world as people strive for peace with justice everywhere.

Creating a culture for peace presents both challenges and opportunities for all of us.

The first of these challenges has to do with how we think about and speak about peace. Peace scholars for more than sixty years have accepted peace scholar Johan Galtung's original definition of peace as an absence of war and violence. He refers to the absence of war and armed conflict as negative peace and the absence of personal, community, and systemic violence as positive peace. Concepts of peace as an absence of war or violence have actually limited our ability to imagine, understand, or communicate with others about what peace *is*! Moreover, such concepts have hindered us in our efforts to act together to manifest and sustain a culture of peace.

Let us rethink such widely held definitions of peace as an absence. In my work as an international peace educator, consultant, and coach, I define peace as *"the presence of just and faithful relationships with one self, with others within a family and a community, among all peoples both within and between nations, with all of creation, and with a Spiritual Being/Higher Power who both gives life and gives life meaning".* We can conceptualize peace as present when relationships are just, human rights are respected, the common good is assured, global security is achieved, and actions are informed by a personal and communal commitment to the promotion of family, community, national, and global peace with justice.

By changing our definition of peace, we can begin to imagine, embrace, and celebrate genuine peace as a presence that is—or is in the process of becoming—whole and integral in people's lives. When peace is viewed as a presence, it is experienced as life-giving, freeing, and energizing, with the potential to change both personal and institutional behaviors within local, national, and international arenas.

To achieve a culture of peace, we also need a deeper understanding of the place of conflict in our lives, at the personal level as well as at the community, national, and international levels. Conflicts abound. In an interdependent world, we all face challenges related to understanding and responding to conflicts and acts of violence, terrorism, war, and the social, political, economic, and environmental threats that hamper people's quality of life at the family and community level, as well as at the national and international level.

The existence of conflict can be good because it challenges us to examine choices and options, and to clarify values and goals. It is how we respond to conflict that hinders or enhances our efforts toward peace. Conflicts present us with challenges to be met and problems to be resolved in caring ways, ways that respect the legitimate needs of everyone involved.

Resolving conflict peacefully requires new models and methods of effective communication and problem-solving skills. Intentional and appreciative listening across differences can rekindle our ability to engage in civil discourse at the personal level; mediation, arbitration, and negotiation can lead to problem-solving at the personal and the community levels; and diplomacy and conciliation can help achieve the peaceful resolution of conflicts that affect peoples' lives at the national or international level.

Acts of violence, including acts of armed conflict and terrorism, pose a different set of problems for all of us. Violence consists of any intentional behavior that causes harm to another, and includes any act—physical, emotional, verbal, or psychological—that threatens or forces a person or community to act in ways that right reason, law, or moral suasion could not. Systemic or institutional violence and injustice occur when basic human and civil rights and freedoms are denied others based upon public law or policy, or corporate or community practice. Systemic violence affects groups of people rather than just individuals, and is based on practices that discriminate against others because of differences in gender, age, race, national and ethnic origin, religion, marital status, sexual orientation, or ability level.

A commitment to both the theory and practice of nonviolence has been a powerful motivator for those seeking to understand and resolve conflicts peacefully. A commitment to nonviolent action by people who gather to protest unjust treatment and limits to the rights of full citizenship has helped bring about change in unjust regimes, as well as to unjust policies and practices in communities and countries around the world. Growing numbers of people from tribal, religious, racial, ethnic, cultural, and/or political groups who have been in conflict with each other within or between nations have come to recognize the importance of working together for the common good; they have put aside their differences and have directed their energies to meet both group and common goals, and have done so without the threat of force or outside intervention. When these methods are used at national and international levels, such efforts can also help to reduce threats from terrorist attacks, invasion, or warfare, as well as threats from economic exploitation, political oppression, and even genocide.

Identifying and transforming cultural paradigms present yet other challenges. Our paradigms, or worldview, shape how we think about the world and our place in this world, and also how we think about the place of others within this world. A worldview based on racism, sexism, competitiveness, authoritarianism, or domination gives rise to policies and practices that result in economic exploitation, political oppression, the militarization of society, environmental pollution, and the exploitation of human and natural resources. Addressing critical and complex issues resulting from these attitudes in an effective, life-sustaining way for the benefit of all people requires a major paradigm shift. Responsible women and men from all areas of life recognize the links between destructive cultural paradigms and the problems, crises, and challenges that confront and threaten all with global chaos.

Paradigm shift is possible. A worldview that supported slavery, etched into the minds of people and written into the laws of many lands, decreased with the efforts of leaders who worked to abolish slavery in the eighteenth and nineteenth centuries. A worldview that supported colonialism changed as leaders on all continents sought political and economic independence with and for their people. A worldview that fostered discrimination against specific groups of people is changing because leaders are speaking up for civil and human rights and seeking to assure that access to housing, employment, education, mobility, and social and cultural opportunities are available to all. A worldview that has permitted child slavery, environmental devastation, and even terrorism is changing because citizens of the world are speaking up and challenging such practices. Today, both government and community leaders on all continents are directing their efforts away from a worldview that has supported aggression and warfare as a reaction to armed conflicts and are choosing diplomacy and nonviolent action in response to such acts of injustice.

When we are open to changes in our understanding of peace as a presence, and to a consideration of nonviolence as a means to effect change in our world, we can more readily examine commonly held cultural paradigms and declare our commitment to work with others in our communities and our world to establish systems and adopt policies and practices that lead to global cooperation and genuine partnership.

We also recognize that we can only create what we can first envision. History and our never-ending news cycles remind us that some have used their imagination in ways that inflicted incredible evil and harm to others in our world in the form of slavery, warfare, genocide, and the destruction of our environment. We can challenge this by directing our energy toward visioning a culture of peace, leading us to consider new possibilities for a world in peace.

Both within the personal space of family and the public spaces of our global village, the process of creating a culture of peace depends upon how well we choose to live by values that honor relationships and the common good. Values have been referred to as strong beliefs about matters of principle that drive behavior. Moral values are shaped by life experiences within a family, a community, and the wider culture. Both personal and public values are manifested through the activities of our every-day lives. We understand that transforming a culture from one of dominance, violence, and militarism to one of peace with justice depends upon the extent to which we can inspire, empower, and energize ourselves to express personal and public values in all dimensions of life.

We absorb personal values from the experience of living with others in the home and through daily interactions with others in the wider community of neighborhood, classroom and other where people gather. Spiritual and/or humanistic values lead us to acknowledge the presence of a Spiritual Being or Higher Power in our lives and to honor the dignity of each person; personal integrity leads us to honor truthfulness; compassion leads us to work with and for others to alleviate suffering; hospitality leads us to welcome all; generosity leads us to share with an open heart; forgiveness and reconciliation lead us to see conflict as a problem to be resolved rather than a struggle to be won or lost and to heal both individual and community pain; gratitude leads us to acknowledge blessings and gifts received; and cooperation leads us to seek for inclusiveness in our work with others to achieve the common good.

Public values, which build on personal values, are not so much absorbed from the experiences of daily living, but are instead adopted as a conscious decision to treat others and the entire ecosystem in just and peaceful ways.

Public values are manifested in multiple ways during the personal and professional activities of our everyday life. Our commitment to personal and global spirituality leads us to respect the diverse ways that people acknowledge the presence of a Spiritual Being or Higher Power in their lives; our commitment to ecological integrity leads us to honor the earth and treasure its resources and all of creation; our commitment to social responsibility leads us to act in ways that respect the human rights of all people; our commitment to economic equability leads us to assure that all people have a right to equal access to the goods and resources of the earth; our commitment to political participation leads us to protect people's right to engage in decisions that affect their lives; our commitment to a peaceful world leads us work with others to resolve conflicts without resorting to armed force or violence; our commitment to a sense of our shared kinship with others leads us to make decisions that respect our global interdependence; and our commitment to our global security leads us to seek for our common good. In all of these ways, adopting and manifesting public values strengthens our ability to create and sustain a culture of peace in our families, our communities, and in our global village.

Reflection upon the relationship between personal and public values reveals that both connections and tensions exist between and among them. Environmental issues and development issues point to two of these tensions, raising questions about development *for whom, by whom,* and *with whom* and *with what results to people, their communities, and the environment.* Because values themselves are so often in tension, the challenge for those seeking to create a culture of peace is one of finding ways to live creatively with and respond justly to potential conflicts and tensions in our lives. This is why values are so important! They strengthen us in our resolve to live and act as peacemakers with all the myriad people who touch our lives in all the myriad places where we live our lives. Our vigorous and vigilant commitment to embrace and then manifest personal and public values in all aspects of our personal, professional, and public life can help us in our individual and communal efforts to sustain a culture of peace.

We who seek peace also ponder whose voices need to be included in order to reach decisions that will benefit individuals, communities, and the common good. We want to know *who names the participants. Who names the agenda? Who names the issues? Who determines the principles and policies that affect all of life?* We want to know whose voices are missing and whose voices are included and then we seek to insure a diversity of voices in the decision-making processes that affect all of our lives. We recognize that for peace with justice to occur, it is necessary to take time to listen for and to these multiple voices. Worldwide, women, men, youth, and even young children are using their voices and claiming their power, working together to bring healing and wholeness to a hurting world, revealing their potential to bring their vision of peace with justice to reality.

How, though, do we *sustain* a culture of peace for today and for future generations?

Genuine peace occurs only when we make a commitment to *do something*, to engage in just actions needed to create a culture of peace in our world. Every day and in all sorts of ways, people *do something* as they engage in actions related to war or violence. Some do so as part of their daily work experience: planning strategy; funding research; developing and using weapons; training soldiers; engaging in combat; sewing uniforms; preparing the meals for military personnel; reporting the news. Others do so as an unintended part of their civilian life: tending to the wounded; burying the dead; cleaning up the debris; and rebuilding communities. We give these activities a name: military research, military training, military action, even war reporting; or in the case of civilians, providing emergency care and community support.

Peacemaking also calls us to *do something* as part of the activities of our everyday personal, professional, and civic life, too.

Peacemaking activities can take place in the private spaces of our homes with family and friends as we engage in the domestic and nurturing activities of family life as well as in the public places of our communities where we engage in work, play, and service activities of our lives.

Working for peace can take many forms. At the personal and community level, we can engage in activities of direct service through organizations that provide for immediate need, honoring the dignity of the human person. We can advocate in order to influence government and corporate leaders to create systems and structures and to establish and monitor policies and practices that meet human need. We can empower others through education and training. We can stand in solidarity with those facing grave risk. We can care for the earth and its resources to assure sustainable environments for all peoples and their communities. At the government and corporate levels, we can establish and monitor systems and policies that support and protect a culture of peace. Working for peace with justice is as relevant in the government and corporate offices and boardrooms of bankers and manufacturers as it is in the family, the classroom, and the workplaces of our world.

Each of these acts, when done with love and embraced with vigor, valor, and vitality, helps us to connect peacemaking within the family with peacemaking in that broader world where we live, work, play, study, serve, worship, and celebrate.

Our challenge is learning how to name these activities in our home, our community, and our world as peacemaking activities, which can help us work toward both creating and sustaining a culture of peace for today and for future generations.

Peacemaking is a complex, life-long process!

Peace *is* more than just the absence of violence, terrorism, and war. It is the presence of justice—in all of our relationships and throughout all of our lives. By redefining peace as a presence of just and faithful relationships with each other and all of creations, by reexamining our understanding of both conflict and paradigms, by identifying the vision and the values essential for creating a culture of peace, by holding fast to an image of a world at peace, by making a commitment to do something—to engage in just actions for peace—and by naming these activities as peacemaking activities, we can create a culture of peace for our families, our communities, our nations, and our world.

We who are committed to the establishment of peace with justice for all people recognize that peace flows from our ability to use our imagination to vision a culture of peace; to choose language patterns that both name and communicate peace to others; to create systems and structures that can support a culture of peace; to establish legislation and monitor policies and practices that promote, protect, and preserve a culture of peace; to educate ourselves and others both *about* and *for* a culture of peace across the generations; and to act—alone and with others—to sustain a culture of peace. Only then can we hold fast to an image of a world *in peace* and not just a world *not at war.*

Let us, together, join with others in creating and sustaining a culture of peace, one that we can pass on to our own and all the world's children, now and unto the seventh generation and beyond.

The choice is ours.

To contact Jacqueline:

Jacqueline Haessly

Peacemaking Associates

9418 N. Green Bay Road

Suite 366

Brown Deer, WI 53209-1073

Phone: 414-355-9450

Email: jlhpeace@icloud.com

Facebook: www.facebook.com/jacqueline.haessly

Facebook: www.facebook.com/44peace

Denise Needham

Denise's multifaceted career has included sales and marketing for consumer product companies such as Kellogg's®, Carnation®, ConAgra Foods®, and Campbell Soup®; developing government bids and proposals in the aerospace industry; working for the executive team at Quest Diagnostics®; Director of Business Development for FutureKids®, a global franchise offering K-12 curriculum as well as an instructor at Lindamood-Bell® Learning Centers.

More recently, she has spent over 12 years in the direct selling industry as Sr. Director of Training and Field Development leading a talented team earning two of the Direct Selling Association's Education and Business Development Awards while working for Arbonne® International and Beachbody® LLC. Denise earned her Bachelor of Science degree in business management from Pepperdine University, in Malibu, California with a focus on Organizational Development.

She is the founder of ROI Results Oriented Innovation and the Women's Partnering Network, a mentoring program designed to help women enhance their personal life and careers. Denise became a Certified Trainer for FranklinCovey® Leadership programs and for The Color Code® Personality Assessment. Her passion in life is to help others live their purpose acting on what is important to fulfill their mission, and time with her husband, two children, and five grandchildren.

Change with Purpose, Passion, and Power

By Denise Needham

While out on one of my morning runs around the lake, I was going through my usual laundry list of things to do that day and feeling like I wasn't accomplishing as much as I wanted. This often leads me to thoughts where I begin doubting my choices or intense self-examination about why I'm not doing more. But this morning I heard that still voice inside say:

> *"Each day is a gift, now what are you going to do with it?"*

I stopped dead in my tracks and let the love of God consume me. What a loving God He is, to speak to my heart with words that sent such a powerful uplifting message. For the rest of that day, and each day since, I have a new appreciation for His gift.

Looking back over the decades, there have been many changes that have happened in my life, some deliberate and wanted, some unexpected and dreaded, but what I've learned is this:

> *"You can't control everything in life, but you can make choices in every situation that will impact the outcome."*

Having the will to choose how we think, communicate, and interact with others is one of the most powerful gifts we have as human beings. And it's not always easy to do what's best. Even when we try our hardest and mean well, the outcomes don't always go as planned. We entertain bad thoughts or give into emotional hurtful reactions causing regret and guilty feelings for our behavior. Just when we think we are on the straight and narrow path, we fall off due to temptations that overpower us. Where is our *moral compass* when we need it most? How might we control our thoughts, words, and deeds towards goodness? Do we have the ability to change ourselves based on reason alone?

Having been raised in the Midwest in the 1950s, living on the banks of the Mississippi River, one of five girls, I remember having the inner drive to excel at everything. Whether playing or doing chores, I liked doing things right, being the best, and not settling for anything less. But I also remember having had my fair share of spankings for breaking the rules and not doing what I was told.

By the time I reached high school, I knew I was very gifted in music, playing piano, then learning to play guitar and French horn in the band and orchestra. I would try out for the plays and get leading parts with almost no effort, and usually got straight A's in most of my classes. I also wrote songs and loved singing in the choir. My heart soared whenever I was performing. I knew that these talents were my gifts and I had dreams of becoming an actress, singer, and songwriter. But given the circumstances of my home environment, the lack of constructive mentoring and inner spiritual guidance, I made choices that put me on a completely different path. If only I had been given the knowledge and power to choose wisely.

Knowing Your Purpose

pur·pose

/ˈpərpəs/

noun: *purpose; plural noun: purposes*

The reason for which something is done or created or for which something exists

> *"The person without a purpose is like a ship without a rudder."* – Thomas Carlyle

Have you ever asked yourself, "Why am I here and what is my purpose?" Perhaps the first time you did was when you felt the anxiety of trying to decide what you wanted to do after high school graduation. Or can you recall being asked, "What do you want to become for the rest of your life?" Can you remember asking yourself, "Where should I go to college...or should I go to college? Should I stay at home or move out, find a job, or join the military?" Unfortunately, in many cases, young men and women find themselves wandering in a labyrinth of decision making with no purpose, passion, or power to make the right choices.

> *"It's impossible to live a life of passion when we do not know our purpose in life."*

When there is a lack of good coaching, caring mentors, or healthy parenting, we can easily be led astray and end up on the road that leads to living a life of "just getting by." Is that where you see yourself right now? Do you know what your purpose in life is? If not, then I want to encourage you to take the time to consider it. Because once you know and take steps to act according to that purpose, you will begin living a life of abundant happiness and fulfillment.

Having a Trusted Inner Guide

Regardless of your circumstances, upbringing, culture, or lifestyle, there is no guarantee you'll have the guidance early in your life to help you find your purpose. Yet, we do have a trusted inner guide available to each of us. I believe it's a lack of knowing God and not having a personal relationship with Him that leaves us wandering in a hopeless maze of relationships, seeking others and material things to fill a void in our hearts that only He can fill. He is the one who can help us find and understand our purpose.

After years of tragic heartbreak filled with mental and physical abuse, my life changed at the age of 25. My neighbor, who watched my children, spent a year praying for me every day after I was divorced. She had seen me filled with anger, regret, and bitter resentment. Every Sunday morning, she would call and invite me to go to church. I would wake to her call, exhausted from an evening of partying, and would politely decline with another lame excuse. But she never gave up. Finally, one Sunday morning, I decided to take her up on her invitation with the stipulation that she was never to call me again to go to church if I went today. She replied, "Absolutely! I won't call you again if you go to church today." I asked her what time was she going to pick me up, and she let me know she had been to the early morning service, and I would need to drive myself. And I did just that, because I thought it was a small price to pay to be rid of her Sunday morning wakeup calls.

My mother was Catholic, so she took the spiritual lead in our household by taking all five of her daughters to the Catholic Church. When I walked into the Assembly of God church in Bellevue, Nebraska that October morning in 1977, I was not expecting to see bright lights, people standing, clapping, and singing together with big smiles, hands raised high in the air in worship. I made sure I sat in the last row at the back of the church to make a quick escape the minute it was over. However, as I listened to the sermon that morning, I found myself crying uncontrollably. I did not understand what was happening or why, but when the pastor explained that just by asking we could be forgiven for all our sins, I decided at that moment to accept Jesus Christ into my heart.

From that day on, instead of hating God, I wanted to just fall into His arms to be safe and learn whatever I could to live my life based on His plan for me. I wanted to be a better person, mother, daughter, sister, and friend. I knew I couldn't change the past, but I could make better choices for my future by asking for God's help. After all, I knew no matter how hard I tried, I wasn't able to be the person I wanted to be on my power alone. My failures and mistakes were proof enough of that.

So the work began, and still happens every day. I simply spend time studying, praying, and talking with God about everything, out loud as if we were physically sitting together. That's not to say I haven't strayed or ashamedly made choices that were totally against what God so wanted for me…after all He never violates the power to choose freely, a gift that He gave each one of us. But, here is what I have come to experience, something reinforced when I first read Rick Warren's *The Purpose Driven Life – What on Earth Am I Here For*? God has a purpose for each of us. He uniquely gifted us with talents to serve that purpose. When we live out our lives utilizing those gifts in the ways He purposed, we experience love, passion, and true fulfillment.

There is no more guesswork. No longer do you have to ask yourself, "Why am I here, what am I supposed to do with my life, what kind of job should I go for?" Because when you seek Him, and ask for His guidance, He is faithful and trustworthy to show you. You *can* trust God and He will empower you with the ability to succeed.

Pastor Warren has an entire teaching on knowing your gifts that guides you through a series of questions to learn your purpose. I highly recommend this as your go-to resource for clarity around *your* purpose in life.

> *"If you're alive, there's a purpose for your life."* – Rick Warren

Being Fueled by Passion

pas·sion

ˈpaSHən/

noun

A strong feeling of enthusiasm or excitement for something or about doing something

Once you know your purpose in life, you can't help but feel excitement about what you can accomplish each day. No longer will you have to set the alarm and drag yourself out of bed with dread for the day ahead. It's like *recess all day* because it feels more like play than work. The enjoyment you feel as you go about the activities of what you are doing is endless. When there are challenges and obstacles that cross your path, rather than avoid staying engaged, you'll feel the enthusiasm to press forward no matter what happens or how difficult things are.

In one of my most recent positions, I was given the role of Sr. Director of Field Development. Over the years, I have expanded my ability as a speaker and trainer. I fell in love with personal development while attending Pepperdine University in the late 1990s. Being able to help people be better at what they do resonated with the desires of my heart. After working in sales and marketing, and advancing in positions that required me to train sales representatives and managers, this newly developed role felt natural and rewarding. So in 2009, I took the Sr. Director position at Beachbody in Santa Monica, CA. Along with helping to develop business tools, my position changed to Field Development Trainer. This required me to fly each week to markets in the US and Canada to conduct training to groups of 50 to 500 distributors and on the main stage at the annual sales events before thousands.

Even though there was extensive travel, oftentimes days where I would not only be away from home, sleeping in countless hotels, waiting through delays at airports, and dealing with the time change and weather conditions, I loved what I did so much that none of the difficulties mattered. People would often say to me, "You always have this great smile, you seem so happy and full of so much energy…how do you do it?" and my answer was always the same, "Because I love what I do." This love for what you do is what fuels this strong feeling of passion.

If you are not feeling enthusiasm and excitement over what you are doing, then it's time to ask yourself, "Why not?" Have you allowed yourself to become complacent and comfortable in the day to day, only to find yourself not really caring anymore? Have you fallen into the trap of fear, not wanting to step out in faith finding your passion and following your purpose? Then it's time for a change, and only you can decide. Don't be afraid to ask for God's help, He will never let you fall. Stop the excuses. Seek, ask, trust—and change will happen.

> *"Passion is energy. Feel the power that comes from focusing on what excites you."* – Oprah Winfrey

The Power to Succeed

pow·er

ˈpou(ə)r/

noun

Ability to act or produce an effect; capacity for being acted upon or undergoing an effect; capability of doing or accomplishing something

> *"Nothing can withstand the power of the human will if it is willing to stake its very existence to the extent of its purpose."* – Benjamin Disraeli

Ask anyone "what is power?" and you will get different answers such as: knowledge is power; information is power; strength is power; money is power; vision is power…all of these are true, and can influence dramatic changes to occur. To bring about human development, we need that power to act or produce a change to come from within.

In the 1980s, I was struggling to keep some extra pounds off, and decided I would start running for exercise. The first goal was to run for one mile around the housing track in Olathe, KS because it was nice and flat. Getting to that first mile marker was a killer, after years of doing nothing. Once I was able to accomplish it, I decided to continue running daily for a minimum of five days a week. After a couple of weeks, I did not see any weight loss, so I upped the ante to two miles a day. I had to get up a half hour earlier to keep on time for work, and in no time I was hitting that benchmark. Yet, the weight was still not budging. I aimed for three miles a day, seven days a week and I started seeing the pounds slowly come off and I was back into my business suits comfortably. This was my new routine for over two years until I was promoted to the position of Zone Manager for No Nonsense Fashions in Chicago.

The evening I arrived at the hotel in Schaumberg, IL for my training, I was invited by my new boss to join him for dinner. We discussed the events of the upcoming week and then he said, "So, I hear you are a runner." My reply, "Ah, no, not at all, I just run three miles a day to keep my weight off." He responded, "Great! Meet me downstairs at 6:00 am and let's go for a run before we head out." Are you kidding! I was scared and immediately started to panic because I knew he was a ten-time Boston Marathon runner…how in heaven's name was I going to keep up with that? After heading out for our run in the below freezing January weather, we talked business throughout the entire run. When we returned to our starting point, he said, "So how far do you think you ran?" I answered, "Three miles." My boss looked me right in the eye and said, "You just ran six miles." I looked right back at him and said, "No. I run three miles." He remained firm, and restated that I had just run six miles and that's when the epiphany hit me…I could do more than I thought I could, and the only person limiting what I could do was me, and I was doing this by the expectations I was setting on myself. I vowed right then and there never to do that again.

What had started as a weight loss goal turned into a life-changing event. The power I received as a result of that realization led me to complete my first marathon in 1989 in Los Angeles, CA. It only took one year of vision, goal setting, and focus through daily activity to make that happen. The depth of that decision had a much broader and unimagined impact. Each day I went out for a run, I asked for God's wisdom and knowledge. I had my talks with Him on my runs, which were now over an hour. I gained better health and fitness on the outside, and on the inside my heart and mind grew more intimate in relationship with God. Fear and anxiety took a back seat to my willingness to accept changes: a move to a new city; working for a new boss; finding a new home; new schools for the kids; new church and new friends. Where did the courage come from to embrace all these changes?

1. **Knowing Your Purpose** – When you know why God made you the way He did, with your specific talents, and you believe you are part of an entire universe of purpose; you no longer rely on your knowledge or willpower to make choices. You rely on Him to provide. Your confidence is in your creator and what He is capable of, not your limited life's teachings.

2. **Having a Trusted Inner Guide** – Spending time each day talking with God will change your life as you come to know how much He loves you. He will provide whatever you need. As you trust Him, you will be able to trust others. Your relationships and every aspect of your life will change in ways you dreamed and longed for.
3. **Being Fueled by Passion** – Once you start using your gifts, you will find the energy, excitement, and capability to achieve tremendous accomplishments generating complete fulfillment.
4. **The Power to Succeed** – As you connect your will to your purpose, you will find the power to succeed in your life and impact the lives of others.

Luke 1:37—For with God nothing is ever impossible and no word from God shall be without power or impossible of fulfillment. – Amplified Version

My prayer for you is that you will not hesitate to act on these principles and that your cup will overflow with joy and that you will receive unlimited blessings as you allow God a place in your heart.

For more information about Denise Needham's work visit her website and blogs:

Website: www.resultsorientedinnovation.com

Facebook: https://www.facebook.com/pages/Denise-Needham/450864631725652?ref=bookmarks

LinkedIn: www.linkedin.com/in/deniseneedham

YouTube: www.youtube.com/c/DeniseNeedham

Email: 4roi@att.net

DaKara Kies

DaKara Kies is a gifted intuitive healer that specializes in clearing core issues and blocks that hold you back from stepping into your true power, passion, and purpose and working with the inner child to bless, heal, and nurture that most sacred part of ourselves.

DaKara is a healer's healer, assisting healers and light workers to clear the blocks to bringing their gifts to the world. It is time for you to transform the very essence of your being into a radiant and magnificent beacon of light so that your divine purpose unfolds into the richness of your life journey.

DaKara has trained for over 20 years in several healing modalities, and supports her clients on multiple levels, through one-on-one sessions, teleclasses and workshops.

As a Heart Point Technique Master; Certified Energy Healer; and Inspiration, Money, & Relationship Coach, her mission is to share universal healing light with as many people as possible. Light is an alchemical healer that supports each of us, especially in times of transition. DaKara's gifts easily help you shift into your magnificence.

Allow DaKara to guide you in standing in your spiritual authority, so the beautiful light within you can radiate forth to the world.

How to BE Money

By Dakara Kies

Money is simply energy. The word Money has such power—the power we've given it to rule and control our lives or to support and nurture us. Money seems easy when we have it, or does it? When we accumulate wealth, then a possible 'chore' is at hand on how to manage it and what to do with it, where is the best place to invest it, oh the infinite possibilities that having money can bring. Over my lifetime, there have been times when I've had money and not had money. Having money has always been easier for me, as I assume it is for most people on the planet. Having, receiving, and embracing money helps us in multitudes of ways. Having our basic needs met and knowing that money is there to take care of those needs feels like a blessing. When we shift our minds from 'not having' to 'having', we open the doors to magic and unlimited possibilities with money.

It is my intention as you read this chapter that the energies infused within the words move into your energy field to assist and support you in a multitude of ways. At the end of the chapter, I will share how to go deeper into this work.

What happens when you feel you are always in a place of 'struggle' with money? Have you tried and tried to figure out what is 'wrong' with you, why is the money not flowing, what is holding you back, why can't I get a break in the world? Sound familiar? Have you ever had any of those thoughts?

What if the challenge with flow isn't your fault? What if you have what I refer to as a Gatekeeper or Portal Keeper, vows or contracts holding you back from being in the flow with money.

In the transformational energy healing work I share with others, I have observed a theme or challenge around money, and for many beautiful souls, it still is a challenge. Within this chapter, I will share with you some ideas, concepts, and tools to transform these possible 'keepers' or energies that are keeping you stuck in the energy of struggle with money. I will also offer a short meditative experience to assist you in activating your vibrational frequency with money.

So what is a Gatekeeper? A Gatekeeper can be many types or forms of energy. It can be an energy that was created in a past life or from your ancestral line. It can be from traumas in this lifetime or something your sweet inner child experienced. Sometimes thought forms, entities, and discarnates compile to create a Gatekeeper. The great news is, we don't have to figure out what kind of Gatekeeper it is, just that there's something there blocking when it comes to your receiving. Energies carried forward in your family line from ancestors that struggled with money or lived through the Great Potato Famine for example. It could be energies from past lives where you were betrayed in some way around money, or had a powerful life with money or wealth and misused it or held it over others. Most Gatekeepers (about 95%) feel they are protecting you from something. In the above noted examples, a Gatekeeper wants to protect you from experiencing those energies again. Another example might be the energies and words spoken around money in the household you grew up in. "Money doesn't grow on trees" seems to be a popular statement shared in many households. Think of a time as a child when you really wanted something, perhaps an item you saw on TV or in a catalog. What was the response from your parent or guardian when you asked? Many of us heard, "we can't afford that" or the previous statement or something similar. Words have powerful energies and can create a thought form of energy. This can become a Gatekeeper over time, by thinking it is safer to not have or receive so that the energy of 'disappointment' is not a welcomed guest in your heart. Speaking of the energy of disappointment, I know that for me as a child that I was disappointed when I didn't get what I wanted. I believe that this is a normal human response. The energy of disappointment layered with the words and energy and perhaps fears of the person speaking can create patterns and neural pathways, especially when aligned with other energies from past lives or ancestors.

So what is a Portal Keeper? Portal Keepers are energies or beings that either hold open or close a space of energy. A great image that my guides shared with me is a beautiful velvet bag, perhaps filled with coins or some tangible items, the drawstrings at the top are pulled tight. Portal Keepers tend to keep the strings pulled really tight so nothing really gets in. In transforming a Portal Keeper into a Portal Master, an energy that actually helps us to allow the flow of the vibrational frequency of money.

I invite you to visit the link at the end of this chapter to be guided in a grounding exercise, stepping into a sacred healing space as well as a short process to assist you in BEing Money.

Tapping, to come into Balance, is a tool you can use every day, several times per day, to assist you in feeling more peaceful and balanced. You will also hear me chanting ancient languages on some of the recordings. The sound frequency taps into a sound signature around the planet. Some of the words I chant have been on the planet for over 6000 years, just imagine how powerful tapping into that sound signature is! Chanting supports moving the light and energy as well as amplifies their intensity. I recommend checking these tools out before moving deeper, or continue reading and then come back and read the processes I am about to share with you and compare your experiences before and after using the additional tools.

Let's get started! Imagine stepping into a beautiful meadow, surrounded by a circle of sacred healing light. Ground yourself to

Mother Earth by visualizing a cord of light moving from the base of your spine deep down into the core of Mother Earth. Visualize the energy from Mother Earth coming up your spine and into your heart center, send that combined energy up and out of your crown, and imagine it flowing all the way out to Source. Bring Source energy back down into your crown and down into your heart. Take a deep breath in, aligning and anchoring the energies of Mother Earth and Source within your being.

Place your hand over your heart and focus on your high self-point (about 18-20 inches above your head). I will now call forth the light and energy needed to illuminate where you may have energies holding you back. "I call forth the light of illumination, the light of Divine revelation, the sound, color, frequency and sacred geometry that is right and perfect in this moment." Imagine and allow this package of light to flow down into your crown chakra. Imagine it moving counter clockwise through your crown, down through the mid brain, spiraling down through your throat chakra and into your heart. "I now command this light to shine out to an area within my body that is holding you back from being in the flow with money." Imagine the light spotlighting out to any place in your body. Now ask this 'yes' or 'no' response question. "Is there a Gatekeeper there?" Allow your body and heart to respond, the first visceral response. Keep your mind out of the asking. Most times you will 'get' a 'yes'. You may feel your body pull forward, indicating a yes response. Now ask the Gatekeeper: "What is your purpose?" Wait for the answer. 90-95% of the time, the purpose will be around 'Protection'. Rate the intensity of the stuck energy on a scale of 1 to 10 (1 being no discomfort and 10 over the top); make a note of your number.

Let's shift this Gatekeeper, "Calling forth a seed of love to place in the Gatekeeper's heart." Visualize the seed of love is floating down from the heavens and blessing this Gatekeeper. Express gratitude and appreciation to the Gatekeeper for all of the lessons its presence has shared. Now 'ask' the Gatekeeper what it needs for healing. Allow yourself to be present and allow the information to flow forth. If you got "nothing", I will include that in the next step. Trust that your guides are bringing forth exactly what you need to shift and heal. "I call forth and create on your behalf a beautiful energy package filled with unconditional love, Divine forgiveness, Divine providence and all the energies that are right and perfect (your list and what your guides are bringing forth), including what is needed for 'I got nothing'." Imagine a radiant energy package floating at your high self-point, as we guide it down into your crown chakra, imagine you can hear me chanting "An Nur, An Nur, An Nur" (the light) guiding this energy down into your heart and then sending it out to where the Gatekeeper is living. Archangel Michael is assisting in escorting the Gatekeeper into the violet blue flame. Anchoring this with the Truth "Al-Haqq"! Take a deep breath and focus once again on the area you originally identified. Re-rate the energy. If you still have a high number or feel the presence of a Gatekeeper, start over and complete the process again. There can be more than one Gatekeeper connected to the same or similar issue. Tune into your body, heart, and mind and notice how you may already be feeling different when thinking about money. Feeling lighter overall?

Now let's tune in and see if there is a Portal Keeper around wealth, or around the energy of lack or poverty that might be holding you back or keeping you stuck. Close your eyes and tune back into your heart center where we called forth light of illumination earlier. *"I Command the light to show us where there is a Portal Keeper living in your being that is blocking your flow of money, your flow of sustenance."* Allow the light to float out. Now, tune into where the light is shining within your field. Ask this energy if there is a Portal Keeper holding back your connection to wealth and money. A great visual, as noted above, is if you think about a drawstring bag, you may also be observing something similar. The fun in all of this is we are each different and receive information differently, just allow whatever comes. Observe as the bag or object is open, closed, or partially open. What does it feel like? Rate the energy of how open this portal feels on a scale of 1 to 10. How open or closed to the flow of abundance and sustenance. Make a note of the rating. Now ask the Portal Keeper if it is willing to transform into a Portal Master, yes or no? If the Portal Keeper is ready, able, and willing to become a Portal Master, excellent! If you get a no, we will call forth the energy to create a new Portal Master.

Now let's transform the Portal Keeper by creating an energy package that is right and perfect to transform the Portal Keeper into Portal Master. A Portal Master's job is to keep that portal open. Now, if there is some kind of an energy or situation that isn't in alignment for your highest and best, then the Portal Master, of course, would just say, "Halt, no, you cannot enter" but it's going to keep the flow of the energy open for you in a whole different way than a Portal Keeper does.

> *"I Command and call forth an energy package, on your behalf, to transform your Portal Keeper into Portal Master. Or we call forth the energy of a new Portal Master to assist you in being in the flow of money, wealth, and sustenance. To lovingly support you by allowing you to be in the Divine flow with ease and grace. Where you are can BE the energy of money."*

Now imagine the magnificent Portal Master energy package filled with love, a rainbow of color, light, sound, frequency, and sacred geometry, all the energies that are right and perfect for you, flowing down into your crown chakra, *An Nur,* moving it through the corpus callosum (the bundle of nerves that connects both sides of the brain) adding whatever is needed from this package into what will be the new neural pathway, *An Nur,* and allowing it to into the mid brain, *An Nur,* allowing it to float down through the throat and into the heart. Divine Mother is stepping forth with her staff of light as she is taps it on the ground three times, commanding that any Portal Keepers that are not in alignment with becoming Portal Masters are now removed and released into the violet blue flame of transformation and the new Portal Master steps into its rightful place. Imagine the energy package is floating out to your new Portal Master, anchoring in, creating a solid foundation for the Portal Master to stand in its truth, to stand in its power and lovingly support you with BEing money, being in the flow and being open to receive. "Receive the energy of abundance, sustenance, prosperity, the energy of money NOW." Imagine the energy of money is now floating down from your high self-point into your crown. Imagine sparkly gold dust and money energy, allowing it to float down, *An Nur, An Nur,* allowing it to move down into the crown, to the mid brain, into the heart and out to the Portal Master. Observe the Portal Master, how does it feel? Think about money and being in the flow of the energy of abundance and wealth, *Al Haqq*! Take a deep breath in and out. Re-rate.

This work goes much deeper by asking the subconscious mind questions and receiving answer using Dominate and Non Dominate handwriting exercises. Here are some of the questions covered in the class I taught on BEing Money.

What does the energy of lack and poverty have to share with me?

What part of me is benefitting by not allowing money to flow in my life?

Do I have a vow of poverty?

Do I have a contract with the vow of poverty?

Do I have a vow of propensity with lack?

Do I have a contract with the vow of propensity around lack?

Vows and contracts take on a life of their own and can hold you back from all the good the universe has to offer each of its beloved souls. Visiting the Hall of Records and calling forth these contracts and vows and releasing them completely can change your life for the better. Imagine moving into complete flow with money after a few simple processes and the release of contracts and vows.

In the links at the end of the chapter, I have a special offer for you. If you heart is calling you to go deeper and learn more about what is holding money hostage from flowing into your life, then visit the link and take action.

Let's take a meditative journey to anchor in and activate your true BEingness with Money.

Imagine that you are standing in the meadow as I call forth beloved Lakshmi. Imagine her beauty and grace as she walks towards you in her orange, pink, and golden sari, observing the energy of wealth, beauty, and sustenance all around her. Look deep into her eyes, as she places the palm of her left hand onto your third eye. I call forth and create an energy package at your high self-point, filling it with the energy to activate the brain and to create that new neural pathway. Calling forth wealth, abundance, and the energy that will vibrationally and magnetically charge this pathway within your brain to attract wealth, opportunities, and wisdom to utilize the wealth in the best ways for your life. As Lakshmi holds her left palm on your forehead, we're going to drop this energy package down into the crown, *An Nur, An Nur, An Nur*, allowing it to move into the brain, through the corpus callosum, *An Nur,* sparks of light activating the neural pathway, magnetizing it now. Moving it to the back of the head into the consolidation point, *An Nur, An Nur*, allowing it to float down the spine, opening up the chakras to receive this energy activation. Allowing the energy to flow, activate, and energize the neural pathway and any areas of your brain that are connected to the energy of wealth, abundance, and sustenance.

Now we'll install a cord of light that you can use as a tool. Imagine a beautiful, silver orb dropping from your high self-point into your crown, filled with the energy of money, sustenance, and wealth; it unfurls into a cord that spirals down the core of your being, moving down into Mother Earth and anchors between your feet, pulling it taut from the crown to beneath your feet. Visualize you are reaching into your heart and gently strum that cord of light, of wealth, sustenance, the energy of money and just pluck it with your fingertips as if it was a cord on a harp, allowing the vibrational frequency to move throughout your being, into your cells, DNA, RNA, and the subatomic particles within your being. Take a deep breath in and out, drinking in the vibrational energy from the cord.

Raise your vibration by strumming this cord daily to keep the vibration of wealth and the neural pathway magnetized to its fullest status.

I am honored you have taken the time to read this chapter. May you be blessed in all areas of your life.

Resource page for this chapter www.HPTHealing.com/TheChange

To contact Dakara:

Contact DaKara Kies

Websites: www.HPTHealing.com and www.DaKara.com

Phone: 425-267-9730

Skype: DakaraKies

Facebook: https://www.facebook.com/DakaraHPTMaster

Twitter: https://twitter.com/DakaraKies

Jennifer Ritchie Payette, MBA

Jennifer is an intuitive consultant, life coach and entrepreneur. She created a balanced, healthier way of living and working by creating "modules" of horizontal income with a flexible, balanced lifestyle. Jennifer shares her journey in "Modular Career Design-- How You Can Diversify Your Income for the New Economy."

Jennifer has spent her career building, transforming and innovating organizations. She is an expert in strategic planning and organizational development, marketing, social media and distance learning.

An alumnus of one of the world's leading global consulting firms, Jennifer is distinguished by awards in leadership, new product development, project management, marketing and strategic planning. She was Advisory Board Member for Smart Women are Networking (SWAN). Earlier, she was VP Membership and Communications for the DC Chapter of the American Marketing Association.

Jennifer holds an MBA in the Management of Science, Technology & Innovation from The George Washington University and a BA in Economics, International Affairs focus, from Trinity University, San Antonio, Texas. She was an MBA professor.

Jennifer holds numerous certifications including energy balancing, strength & conditioning, healthy lifestyles, and facilitating teams. She was a swim coach, indoor cycling coach, arthritis and fitness trainer.

My Search for Authenticity

Jennifer Ritchie Payette, MBA

I'm a left-brain trained MBA who learned to drive on the right side of the road. I remodeled my lopsided self into a more balanced, joyful human being. I now lead with my heart, looking upward with faith and courage. I now feel significantly more inner peace and joy.

I've always had a desire to help others and I'm highly intuitive. I sense things that remain obscured to others. Like most people, I allowed my ego -- not my heart – to drive my choices so my radar was fogged up. Propelled into ego-driven work instead of heart-centered work, I numbed my heart and wore layers of self-protective armor just to survive.

When I lost my Dad and my job within the same brief period, my ego propulsion collapsed and I felt a seismic shift. My heart opened like a vault. Left with nothing but the prospect of rebuilding, I decided to stop ignoring my inner signals.

Traveling into the center of your being is like venturing into the center of the Earth while simultaneously opening up and out to The Universe. Repeatedly asking yourself "Is this a heart-driven or an ego-driven choice?" launches a surprising journey.

The idea of change triggers fear in most human beings. Looking within is even scarier. Fear causes restriction. It creates boundaries that trap energy. Progress is blocked. Organizations become dysfunctional, stagnant and unproductive. Communities cease to thrive, and need economic development. Cultures bind their people in outdated practices. Ancestral chains pass on grudges and wounds from one generation to the next. All from fear, blocking energy.

I help individuals and organizations reflect, rebalance and move forward. Not to be confused with "curing," the process of "energy healing" removes one roadblock after another. I clear paths blocked with physical, mental and emotional rubble. Energy is both masculine and feminine. It's active and it's also contemplative and reflective. If energy is properly balanced, people smooth out—like rough stones being polished in the ocean. Energy can flow again, freely, creatively and productively.

I hope my story inspires you to take a chance at becoming your authentic self. In doing so, you will unleash your energy to flow freely and naturally, in the direction of your life's true purpose!

Starting Out

The Washington DC area is a tough place to grow up. Parents have big credentials, dual incomes and important careers within mammoth organizations that impact the entire world. To a little kid, that's way beyond reach.

I roamed freely in our community with a strong pack of friends. I had two wingmen who watched my back: one male; the other female. After junior high school, a line was drawn down the middle of our town. We were ripped apart and routed to different high schools that would develop an intense football rivalry, causing us to choose sides rather than build bridges. I lost one of my wings to the rival school, and had trouble flying.

Like everyone, I experienced tough challenges. I was bullied and I survived a major car crash. As a young woman, it never occurred to me to complain or ask for help navigating these ordeals. I found solace in journaling and reading books by motivational coaches such as Dr. Wayne Dyer, whom I viewed as a parallel Dad. Journaling and absorbing positive, uplifting ideas became vital to my emotional survival and personal growth. I poured out my feelings trapped under armor. I thought of this as "processing" my energy. I still do.

I avoided TV; it was too toxic for someone so empathic. Ads portrayed women as shiny cheerleaders. Sitcoms portrayed women as vapid husband-hunting sidekicks. The evening news was the worst; it was sensational, unsettling and scary.

Our family experienced challenges, but I had loving parents who did their best. We had small wardrobes, but left the house with polished shoes and high-quality, ironed clothing designed for longevity.

The most valuable training I ever received in cross-functional team leadership and collaboration never came from formal schooling; it came directly from my Dad, a world class leader who listened to every imaginable motivational guru. He voraciously read numerous books simultaneously, a habit I mirror to this day.

My Mother is a strong, educated female who successfully balanced work and family. She prepared healthy dinners every night. We always ate together, as a family. I learned about DC office politics at the dinner table. She had a VP Finance job, and taught us fiscal responsibility. I started working at a young age and had numerous and varied jobs.

Both my parents valued equality. We shared household tasks, working every Saturday as a team. When finished, we were free to play. Our community was culturally diverse and everyone was welcome in our home. One of the most important lesson my parents taught me was to be a giver, not just a taker.

Launching Ambitions

I sold tickets and popcorn in a movie theatre when "Saturday Night Fever" was released. This triggered fantastic trips to Georgetown, dancing to disco and Motown music. I met my first college roommate at the theatre. We climbed the Washington Monument, engaging in political debate. Behind the silly college motto "We're young, we're good looking and we're HERE," was fiery ambition to make a difference in the world. We later both earned advanced degrees from George Washington University. We also ran a 10K race, promising to finish together. During the race, we became separated. I backtracked, found her, and we finished as a team.

In Washington, DC the prevailing mindset centered on power, BMWs, and angular, leather briefcases. I designed marketing campaigns touting "power" for a leading commercial real estate brokerage firm. I reveled in the emotional dramas called "Doing Deals." The creativity of marketing fed my true self, but I had to prove my worth as a marketing engine driving sales. I learned to focus on numbers and strategy.

This was a wonderful job. The corporate culture fed my soul. The owners treated me like gold, rewarding my accomplishments with flowers, engraved plaques, financial raises, heartfelt hand-written thank you notes and birthday cards. I had a beautiful, plush office with custom wood furniture and stunning upholstery.

My bosses had exceptional emotional intelligence. One planted a seed in my heart that would inspire me to later become a Masters swimmer and coach. These men led with their hearts, not just their minds. They fostered a sense of healthy competition, mutual support, and collaboration.

We were a tightly-knit work family. I felt safe, respected as an equal, and supported. I loved it there. When our paternalistic leader suddenly passed away, the company dismantled and we were all devastated. There was an outpouring from our community at his funeral. This emblazoned an image of the type of person I wanted to be—someone who fed the community with heart-led service.

The Value of Community Service

I had an inspiring coworker there; a former pro football player. He was our star broker. I watched in awe as he threw himself into the world each day with a gale force, then rolled back in like a tumbleweed in a dust storm.

This giant man was like a life coach. He taught me to connect with the community through service. He unselfishly volunteered his time and celebrity to help others in need. Under his armor, his true self was a devoted father, an artist and a humanitarian with a heart the size of the Grand Canyon. Our hearts all broke when he passed away.

Years later, I participated in a competitive cycling event in the mountains. Alone, sweating profusely, I struggled up a steep incline, with pain searing and burning through my legs. I became intuitively aware that my friend was there, coaching me. I could hear his voice, giving me tips. I laughed, thinking I was dehydrated and hallucinating. When I reached the crest, I cried, somehow knowing that life's energy does not end when our physical bodies die; it merely changes form. That is actually a true law of physics. The rest is a leap of faith.

Experiencing Setbacks

My career and life proceeded like a series of grueling football games. I would catch the ball, and run a few yards, just to be knocked down, pushed back, pummeled and bruised. I'd pick myself up, limp along, recharge, then throw myself back in the game, just to be trampled again. A few times I'd score a touchdown, then the drama and agony would start all over again.

I worked like a machine and faced setbacks, including being laid off. One boss said I did the work of 5 people. He was a genius with a big heart who let me work from home when my first child was born. Underneath the machine, my DNA was programming me for healing others from life's challenges.

Real World Lessons

I moved on to a leading consulting firm. I loved the intellectual challenge of working with A-Team stars. My boss was a wise, humble, unmaterialistic man who taught us to never drive a vehicle fancier than the clients who pay our salaries ... unless we wanted to breed resentment.

On Day One, he asked if I wanted to be an "earner" or a "burner." You have to respect his business acumen! Obviously I did not want to be "overhead expense" so I said I would be a "producer." I was so proud to earn a promotion -- and his respect. He was a world class leader with great integrity.

In consulting, when the client needs something, you figure out how to do it. I taught myself how to create strategic plans from a text book before ever completing a single MBA course. My Dad had already planted a seed in my mind that I needed a game plan if I was going to play in the Super Bowl. I had no clue what that meant, but it sounded smart so I became a strategic planner. Today, the Internet allows us to easily access information. You can self-educate if you are resourceful and dedicated to lifelong learning.

Seeking More Balance

I moved to the US Federal government to achieve more balance. I was terror stricken at the thought of Motherhood. Our family physician, a woman, took care to guide me, suggesting I reduce my work hours to create space for children. Her encouragement was crucial and pivotal to my moving forward. She gave me permission to develop my heart and balance my life. I was unprepared for the joy I would experience as a Mother. My life changed dramatically as I started building a family, not just a career.

I envisioned a life similar to Thomas Jefferson's. A childhood trip to the home of Thomas Jefferson's estate Monticello had left an indelible print on me. Jefferson had many different sources of income and varied work roles: he was a parent, a farmer, a master of skilled tradesmen, an inventor, the father of the University of Virginia, and an advocate for freedom. He believed that if a man earned his own bread, he should be allowed to keep it. If he had poor crops, he would survive with income from a side stream.

I started building vertical income for our family and later coauthored a book Modular Career Design to teach this philosophy. I launched a social media movement to encourage others to try a flexible, balanced approach to living. I dedicated the book to an extraordinary college professor who taught me to write clearly.

A Turn in the Road

Later, I worked for a pharmaceutical nonprofit. Our leader was a bold change agent. We successfully blazed new trails there. In parallel, my Dad had become inexplicably stricken. I could only recall him being sick once in his entire life. Just as I had feared becoming a parent, I panicked at the thought of trying to care for my Dad. What did I know about being a nurse? I wasn't trained for this job.

The big recession struck, and I was laid off. I still had my part time job as an MBA professor. I sat next to my Dad's bed, teaching online MBA students worldwide. For the next several months, our family cared for Dad with help from hospice. He passed away in a family home, with dignity, surrounded by his wife, children and grandchildren. There were no hospitals, machines or cold strangers.

I collapsed into bed and felt a sudden deep pain, like a heart attack. I begged God to spare my life so I could take care of my Mother and children. Later, a heart specialist assured me there were absolutely no signs of a heart attack. It was grief.

I organized my Dad's service. I spoke to a crowd without a shred of fear, about this amazing leader and unselfish, generous family man. Golden light poured through the windows, encircling me like a warm blanket. I felt the most profound inner peace. What I didn't realize was that the process of caring for someone to the transitional point of physical death could be as meaningful as the process of caring for a newborn baby entering the world.

Would I do it all over again? Yes. Absolutely. The experience transformed my life and opened my heart. I became a better person with more depth.

A New Life

I took a drastic detour from Corporate America, teaching fitness. I transformed into a swim coach, personal trainer, SPIN instructor, preteen fitness instructor, and an arthritis instructor. I competed in a Chesapeake Bay swim, and completed a rigorous triathlon relay on a "Mom Bicycle." I trained others to be triathletes. Someone I coached said he was motivated by me because I helped him reach for the light rather than run from the cracking whip.

The water naturally attracts people with physical issues. It is a gentle environment. I attracted clients who struggled with serious ailments. They required more time and patience. Occasionally, we sang, to ease pain and fear. I helped broken spirits and bodies. I walked clients to their vehicles. Some I drove over to the subway or to their jobs. Nobody knew I did this. I didn't get paid for it and I earned very little money. It was just the right thing to do. I would never have had the capacity to do this had I not cared for my Dad.

Something inside "clicked" as my heart opened further. Immersed in healing work, I felt surges of energy streaming through my heart, connecting out to my clients. I was completely engaged in the moment and felt joyful and calm. At night, I passed out from so much physical activity. I felt a driving need to do this healing, therapeutic work.

I sought training from world class healers Nadine Mercey, Deborah King and Deepak Chopra. They taught me to lead with my heart rather than my intellect, and to mentally shield myself and detach after helping others to protect my energy reserves. I started creating social media with positive, encouraging messages and calming, inspiring photos. I created an online world to help my clients stay motivated and connected to my energy.

I began experiencing life-altering dreams and awakened to jot notes. Sometimes one to five times per night, as if I were awakening to feed a newborn baby. This went on for at least two years, and continues to this day. Each morning, I'd download my dreams then self-reflect. Through this process, I faced my inner machinations. It became evident that I was finally listening to my own signals that I had squashed my entire life. In trying to heal others I was healing my own self, too.

I released pain and tension, detoxing my body, mind and soul. I started taking salt baths to further detox. I became a vegan. I began feeling profoundly well, whole, calm and free of fear. My senses sharpened even more and I felt connected to everyone. I became more patient, and more intuitively aware of what they needed to release and rebalance.

Along this journey, all the right teachers arrived to guide me on my path. I just needed to keep my faith and focus on love, not fear. When Jim Lutes and Jim Britt invited me to contribute to this collaborative healing project, I knew my prayers had been answered, so I could help inspire change in a more gentle way, on a broader scale. I knew this story should be shared.

I have learned that when we focus on love and strive for balance in body/mind and soul, we experience joy, love, inner peace, wellness, and wholeness. I wish you peace, light and joy as you continue your own journey towards personal transformation.

To contact Jennifer:

https://www.modularcareerdesign.com

AFTERWORD

Life is always a series of transitions… people, places and things that shape who we are as individuals. Often, you never know that the next catalyst for change is around the corner.

Jim Britt and Jim Lutes have spent decades influencing individuals to blossom into the best version of themselves.

Allow all you have read in this book to create introspection and redirection if required. It's your journey to craft.

The Change is a series. A global movement. Watch for future releases and add them to your collection. If you know of anyone who would like to be considered as a co-author for a future book, have them email our offices at support@jimbritt.com.

The individual and combined works of Jim Britt and Jim Lutes have filled seminar rooms to maximum capacity and created a worldwide demand.

The blessings go both ways as Jim and Jim are always willing students of life. Out of demand for life changing programs and events, Jim and Jim conduct seminars worldwide as well as created a global company in over 170 countries called Quanta International that allows anyone to benefit behaviorally as well as financially.

If you would like to hear more about how the Quanta Company can assist you in both income generating and personal development, please email our offices at: quanta@jimbritt.com.

To Schedule Jim Britt or Jim Lutes as your featured speaker at your next convention or special event, email: support@jimbritt.com

Master your moment as they become hours that become days.

Your legacy awaits.

Blessings,

Jim Britt and Jim Lutes

www.ingramcontent.com/pod-product-compliance
Lightning Source LLC
Chambersburg PA
CBHW071903290426
44110CB00013B/1259